Bartosz Beda

Hear My Voice

Bartosz Beda
Hear My Voice

Design
Justin Molloy

ISBN-13: 978-0692855119
ISBN-10: 0692855114

Thank you to Roy, Georgia and Justin for your support in making this catalog happen, and to my wife Nishiki and daughter Yutsuki.

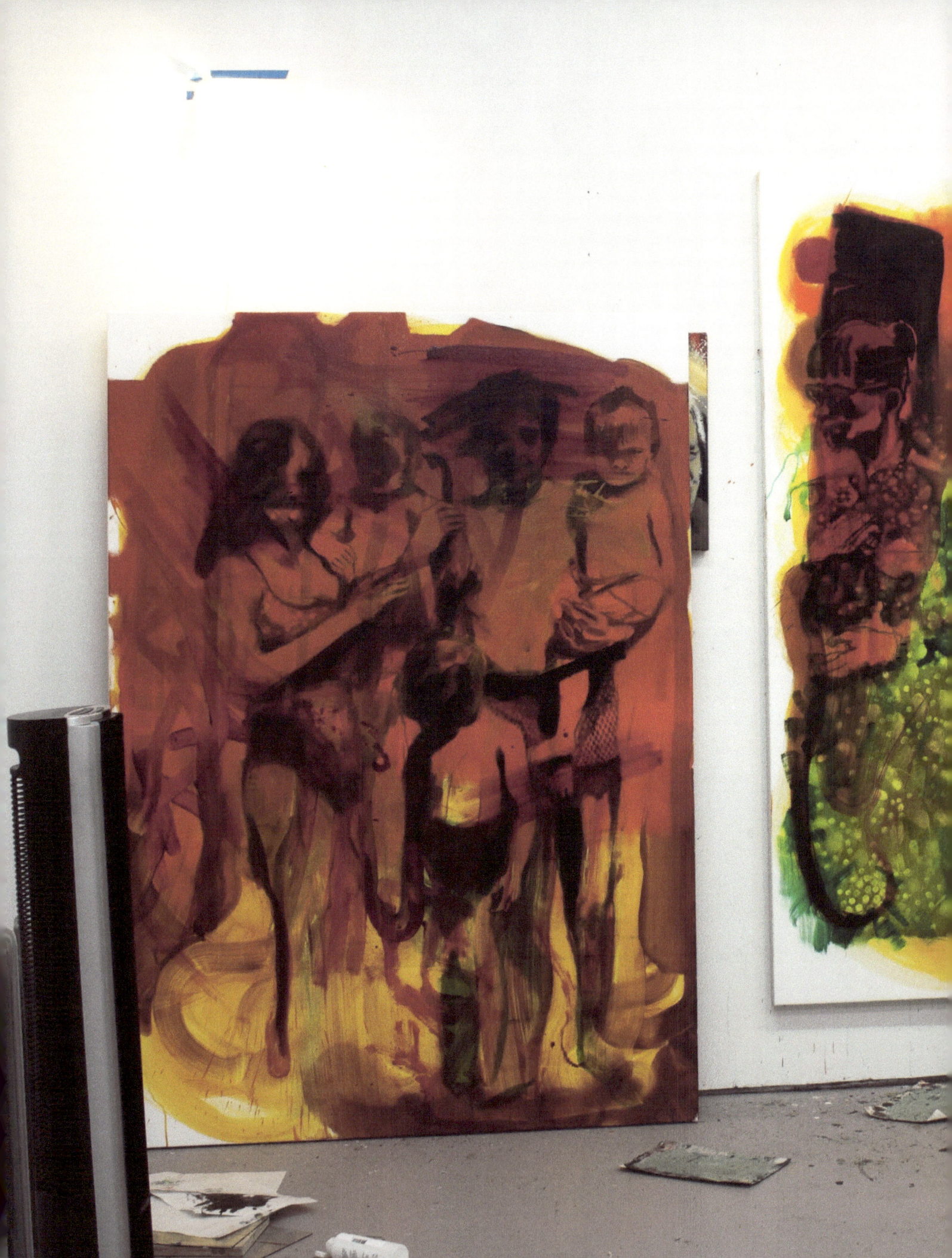

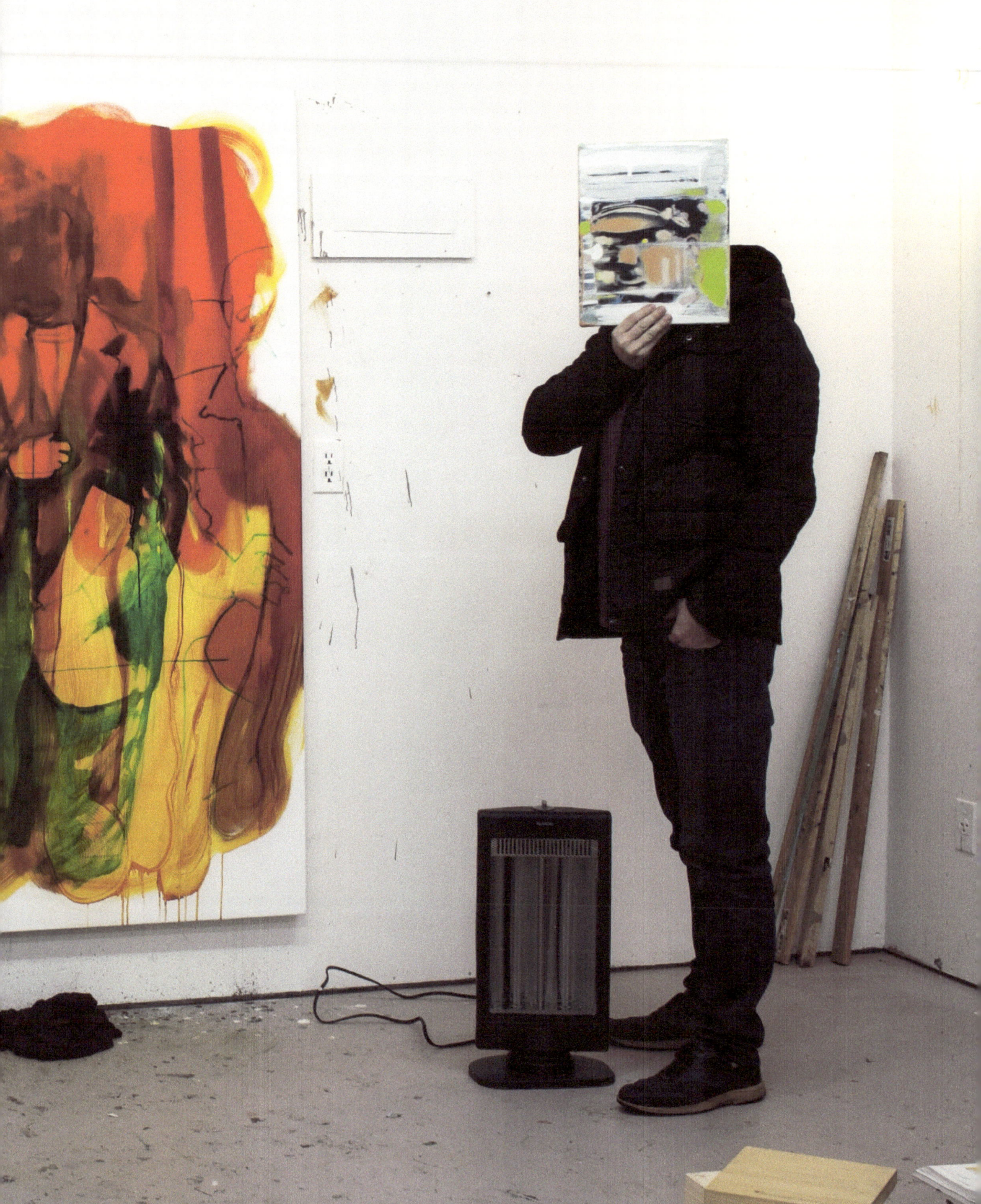

Foreword

Between two worlds
by Roy Sonnema

From the moment of encounter, Beda Bartosz's paintings challenge the viewer. He paints people and figures, but their faces, hands, and bodies are intentionally blurred and masked by anxiously-reworked pigment. He paints spontaneously and expertly building up his imagery, and then deforms it with equal passion. The paintings tend to prevaricate in the viewer's mind, often in troubling ways. How does one explain this?

So much of human experience is a process of our consciousness living within two worlds. One of these is our rational cognitive ability, with which we perceive external reality and try to make common sense of it. In our minds, accumulated sensations, memories and experiences take on a mental order that mirrors reality, provides normative structure, and allows us to think straight.

The other world is that of our internal feelings and emotions, our raw instincts and motivations, which are often hidden from consciousness deep in our hearts. We find ourselves mysteriously attracted to, or repelled by people and things we encounter in the world. Our experiences uncontrollably trigger repressed memories or raw emotions of joy, love, boredom, hate or fear that seem to pull us in all directions.

Bartoz Beda's art is about the liminal space exactly between these two worlds.

In his paintings, we discern vague representational images of heads, bodies, faces, and hands, and we instinctively try to make sense of them. Who are they? What do I know about them? But they are typically unclear or incomplete, resisting identification and representational certitude. The artist manipulates paint, color, and line to disrupt what is seen under layers of expressionist energy and emotion. Faces are obliterated and identities erased under patches of raw paint. Visible hands and limbs move and gesture, but are lost in painterly surfaces worked and reworked with a spontaneous brush.

Each painting becomes a palimpsest of gestural responses layered onto something or someone vaguely seen. They are like provocative half-memories, except that the key visual iconography has been censured by a vigorous brushstroke in wet paint. There is something or someone familiar there, but no matter how much you try to mentally frame it, the associations and emotions flow unregulated in that liminal space each painting opens up.

Few artists today seriously explore this internal space between what we think and what we feel, fewer still do so successfully. Bartosz Beda is one of them.

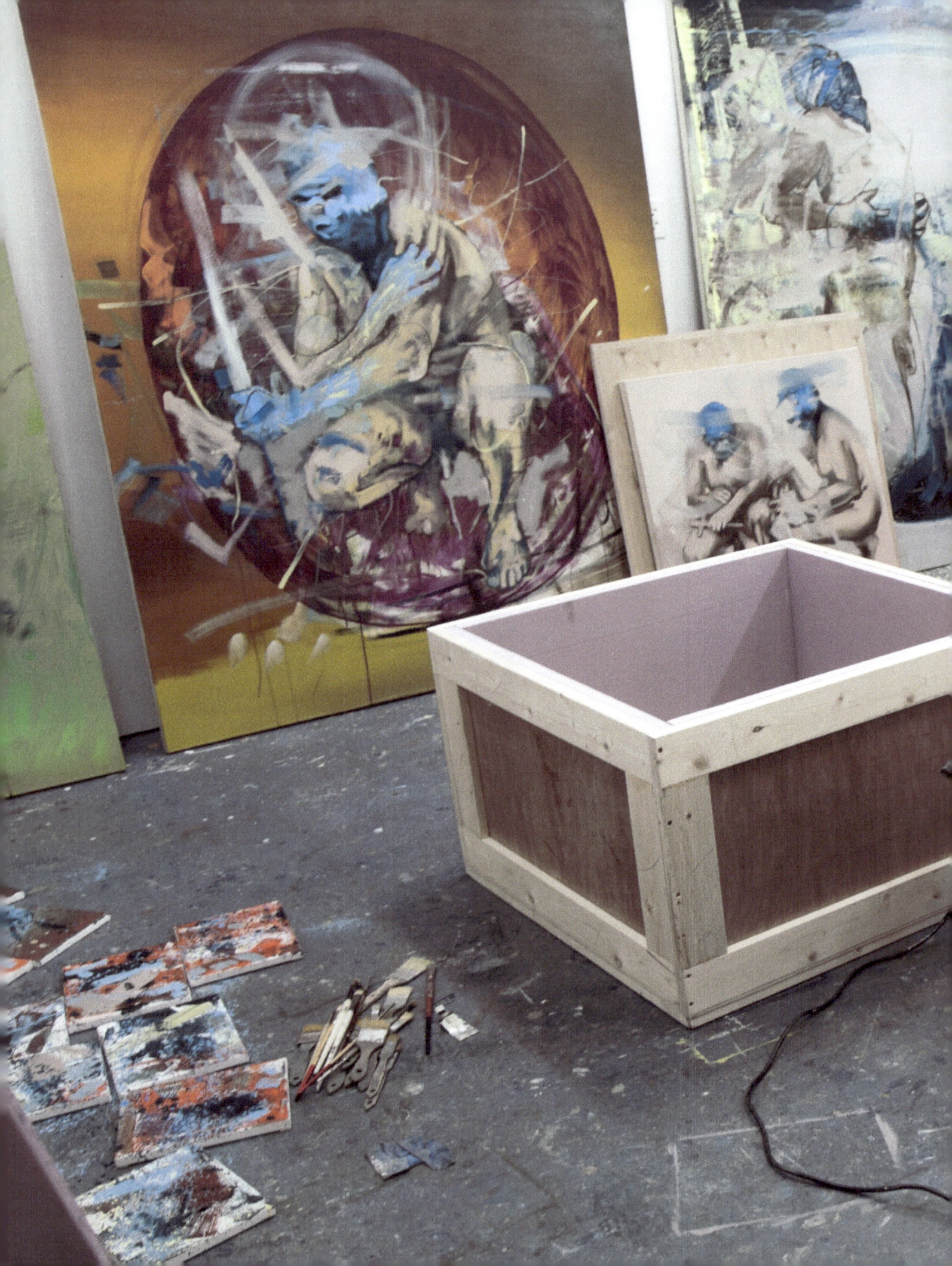

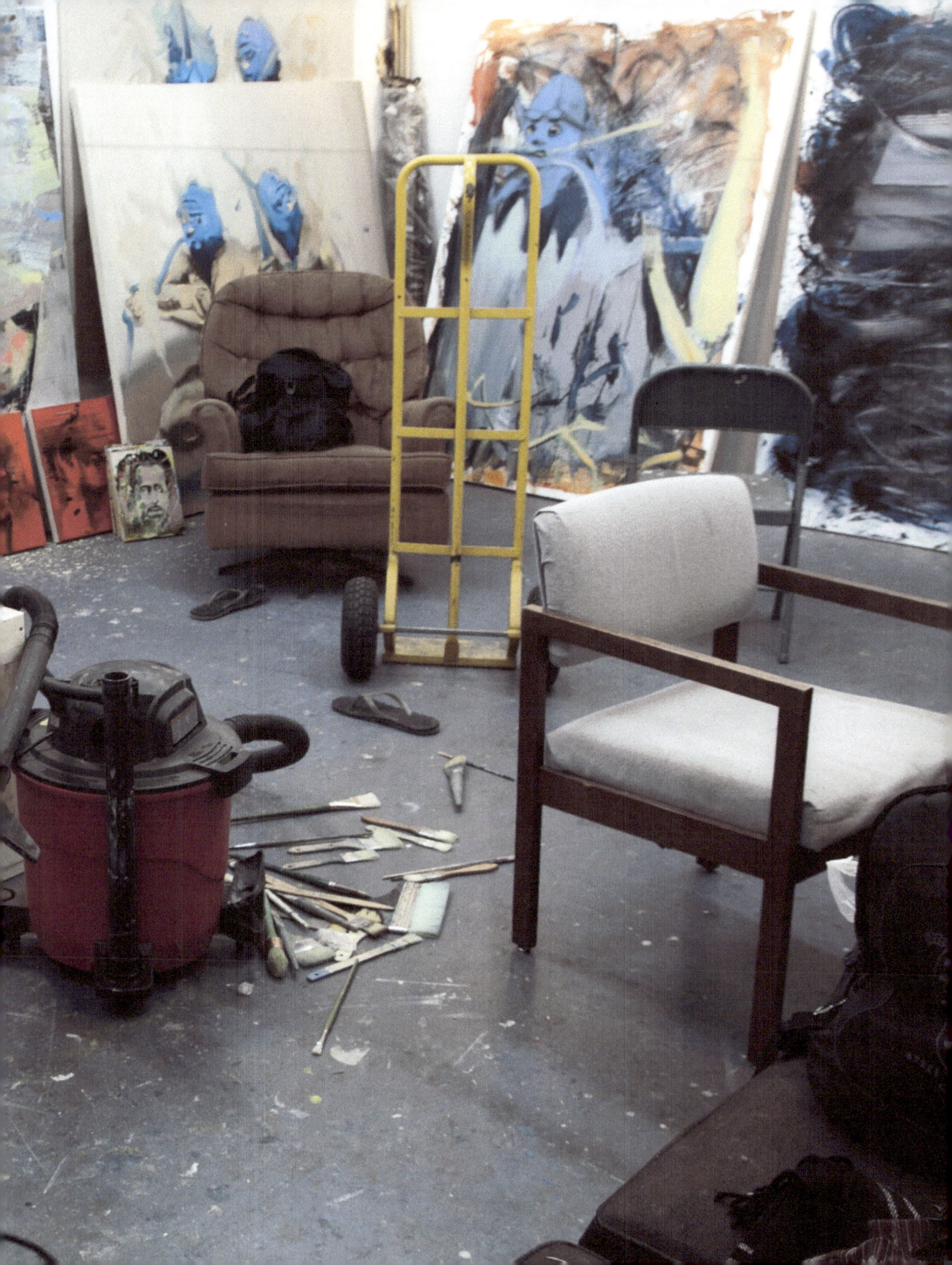

About
the Artist

Hear My Voice

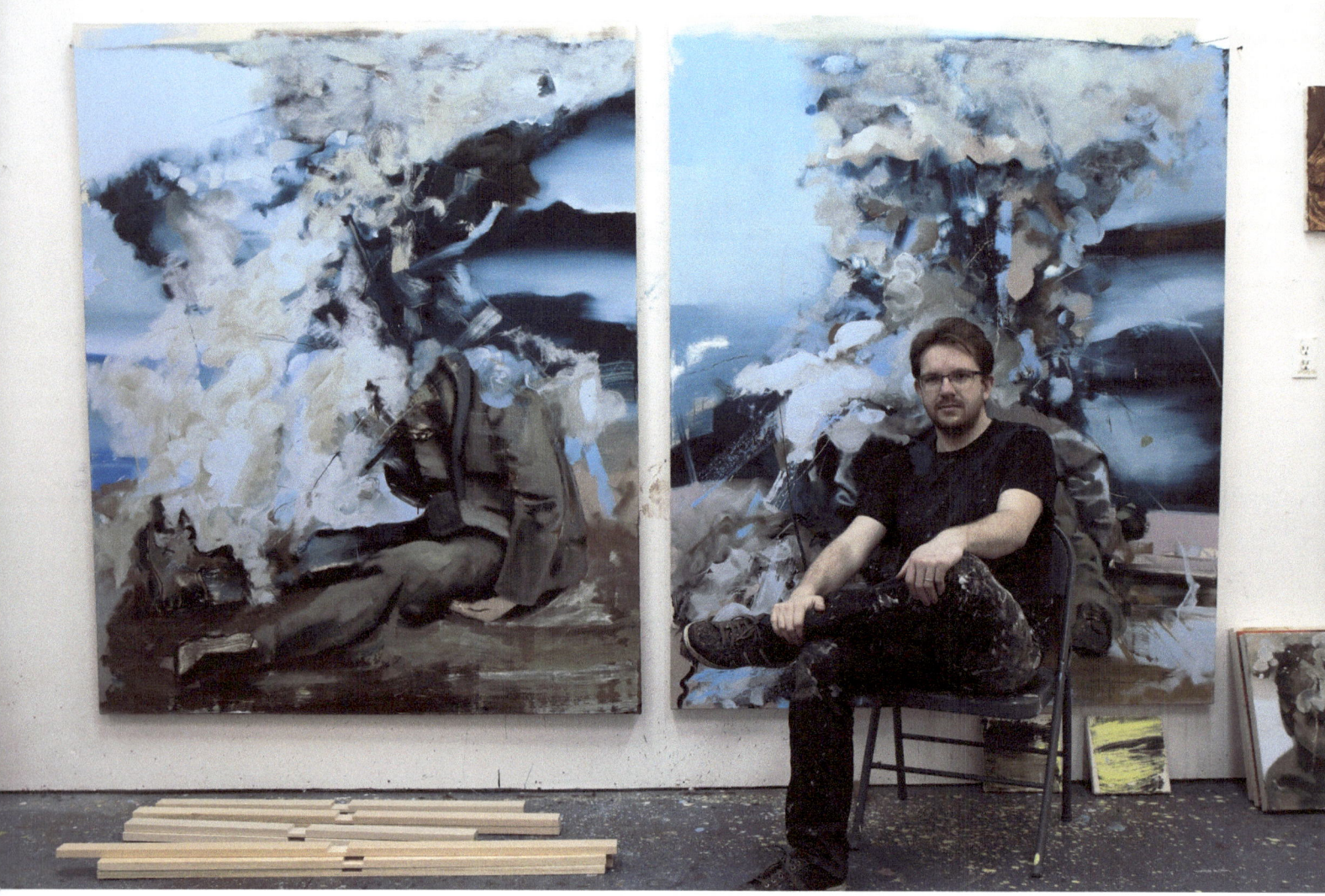

"Bartosz is one of the most exciting early career painters working in the North," says New School House co-director Robert Teed who first exhibited Beda's work in a group show in 2012.

—*Yorkpress, York, UK, March 2016*

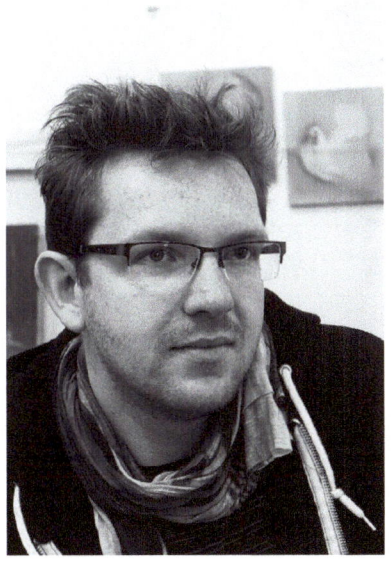

Bartosz Beda
ARTIST BIO

Born in Poland in 1984, Bartosz Beda relocated to the UK in 2008 to study at the Manchester School of Art. After graduating in 2012 with a MA in Fine Art, Beda was selected for the 2012 Catlin Art Guide as the most promising emerging artist in the UK. Short-listed for the Title Art Prize, the Door Prize, and The Saatchi New Sensations 2012, he won the esteemed Torwy Award for the Best of the North of England in 2012. Beda was finalist for the Williams Drawing Prize in Connecticut, USA, and won second place in the Viewpoints 2014 competition at the Aljira, Center for Contemporary Art in New Jersey, USA, 2014.

He was awarded a six-month scholarship from Manchester Metropolitan University to attend the Academy of Fine Arts in Dresden, Germany in 2012-13, and received a fellowship from Fondazione per'l Arte, Rome, Italy in 2016.

Before relocating to England, Beda worked on animation in the film industry, including two movie productions, *Ichthis* by Marek Skrobecki (2005) and *Peter and the Wolf* by Suzieh Tempelton (2006), which received the Oscar Prize in 2007. Beda's art has been widely reviewed and referenced in *The Independent*, *A-N Magazine*, *Mastars at Axisweb*, *Arteon Art Magazine*, *Expose Magazine*, *Spokesman Review*, and featured in *The Guardian*, *The Telegraph* and *Money Week*. Mentioned on BBC Radio 4 in February 2013 as 'one to watch,' he now lives and works in the United States.

For most of his 32 years, Polish painter Bartosz Beda lived in big cities in Europe. He now spends his days painting in the rural Palouse. Shortly after being named as one of Caitlin Art Guide's most promising emerging artists in the United Kingdom in 2012, Beda packed up his paintbrushes and moved from Manchester to Moscow. That's Moscow, Idaho, where his wife teaches art as an assistant professor at the University of Idaho.

In 2013, Beda had planned to visit his then-girlfriend for just a month at her new college town before returning to his busy life and art studio in England. "When I got here I already had my solo exhibition scheduled in Madrid, and I needed to produce more work to fill it," Beda said. "I decided I could just rent a studio here, finish the work, and send it to Spain."

Three years and several international shows later, the artist, who London's Evening Standard calls "a rising star," still rents the same barren studio tucked in a quiet corner of the backyard of a home near downtown Moscow. From a tall table scattered with tubes of oils and cans of drying paintbrushes, Beda works long hours. He's up at 4 a.m., and sometimes paints until 10 p.m., with only the company of a single photo of his wife taped to a wall by a dusty desk littered with tea bags and camera equipment."

—*Spokesman Review, July 2016*

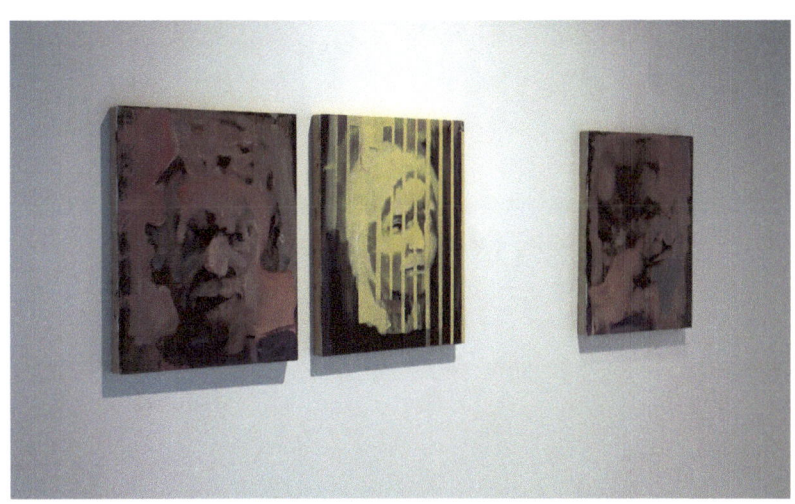

At the age of seven, Bartosz Beda decided to become an artist. Now, just turned 30, he can claim to have fulfilled his childhood dream. He is an award-winning to shows worldwi living out of his pa

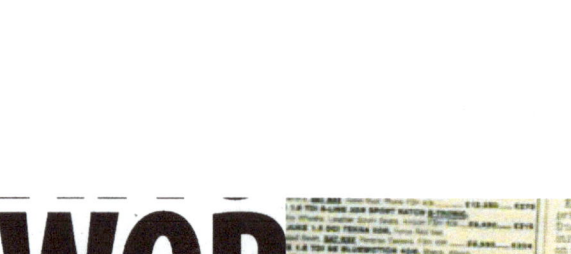

"I studied art in m Poland, which gav and drawing skills in animation until to come to Englan the Manchester Sc art was taught in a representative wa Manchester allowe ment more with id

tutors there, I could develop the conceptual part of my art.

"I was lucky to have my work selected by Saatchi New Sensatio ebsite tha ing artists h their number of me enou e to take ve. n New Jer a show, th Colombia geles. My told me th 95% hard s right."

> *I consider myself a painter of mostly representational paintings, but I also experiment with other forms of painting. This includes a mix of abstraction, figures, and objects, whether they are found or made from a scratch.*
>
> —Alumni Stories, Manchester School of Art

M.E.N. MONDAY, JULY 20,

● Talented Polish

CITY INSP IN THE WOR

Katie Butler
katie.butler@trinitymirror.com
@KatieButlerMEN

MANCHESTER is the most inspirational city in the world, according to a Polish artist who has moved his life to the city.

Bartosz Beda feels so passionately about Manchester that he is willing to be parted from his wife, who lives in America.

The 31-year-old says he does go back to the USA to spend time with his partner but enjoys the city life here too much to leave permanently.

He said: "I studied at the Manchester School of Art and just loved the

main thing I love about Manchester is there are always events going on which makes it very modern and thriving.

"Yet there is so much history based around the industrial revolution. And it's the relationship between the two that I find most fascinating.

"To have this opportunity in Manchester is priceless."

He rents a space in Rogue Studios, off Chapel-

town Road, where he and around 100 other artists create their work.

The building – which was formerly a factory – has been home to artists for the past two decades and celebrates its 20-year anniversary later this year.

"The space here is fantastic, there is so much history to it and it has a story to tell.

"That's what I love about the city. Inspiration is everywhere."

His work has been featured in the Saatchi Gallery in London, with exhibitions in Madrid and Bogota, and he worked on the Oscar-award winning animation Peter and The

'That's what I love about this city.

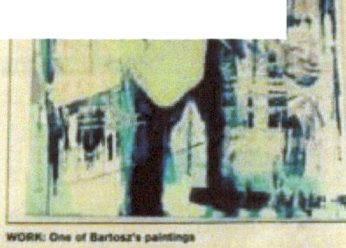

Earlier, he had attended a private fine art college in Poland from the age of 18 to 18 and initially he worked in animation on the Oscar-winning film *Peter And The Wolf*.

After graduating with a BA in Fine Art in 2011, he was selected for the 2012 Catlin Art Guide for most promising emerging artists in the UK and then progressed to the Masters programme at Manchester Metropolitan University.

"Bartosz is one of the most exciting early career painters working in the North," says New School House co-director Robert Teed, who first exhibited Beda's work in a group show in 2012.

Bartosz's most striking works have been placed on the gallery's back wall. "The paintings were based on an article I saw about fashion in the 1920s, in particular about the length that bikinis had to be," he says.

"What aligned in all the pictures was that all the women were looking down when the men were checking the lengths with their measurement tapes as there were strict rules. If the bikini was too short, the girl would be fined."

In creating his paintings, Bartosz started off by using the photographic imagery of the women, then a burst of colours would be applied on top. "I wanted the paintings to express an enjoyment of texture, paint and colour," he says.

Bartosz works in oils. "It allows me to experiment," he says. "You can paint wet on wet, which I like to do, or wet on dry which I also like to do," he says. "Painting wet on wet, I can allow colours to mix; but painting when the paint has gone sticky, I can control it more."

WORK: One of Bartosz's paintings

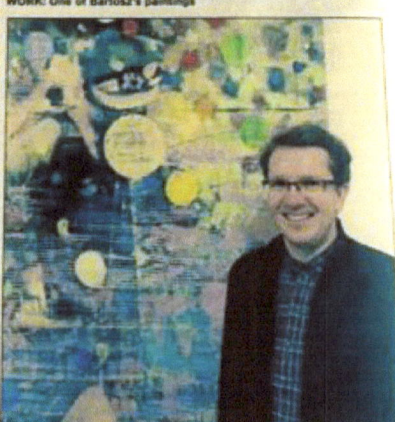

RE-LOCATED: Polish artist Bartosz

Bartosz Beda is a rising star whose paintings reflect social anxieties, with and a keen eye trained on the lessons of history. Beda distils and distorts images garnered through the media, giving them a new vocabulary of tension and threat with his adept handling of paint.

—Studio International

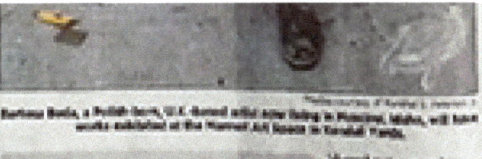

Blast of Absolute Series

Blue Fellow

oil on canvas

178x132cm

2014

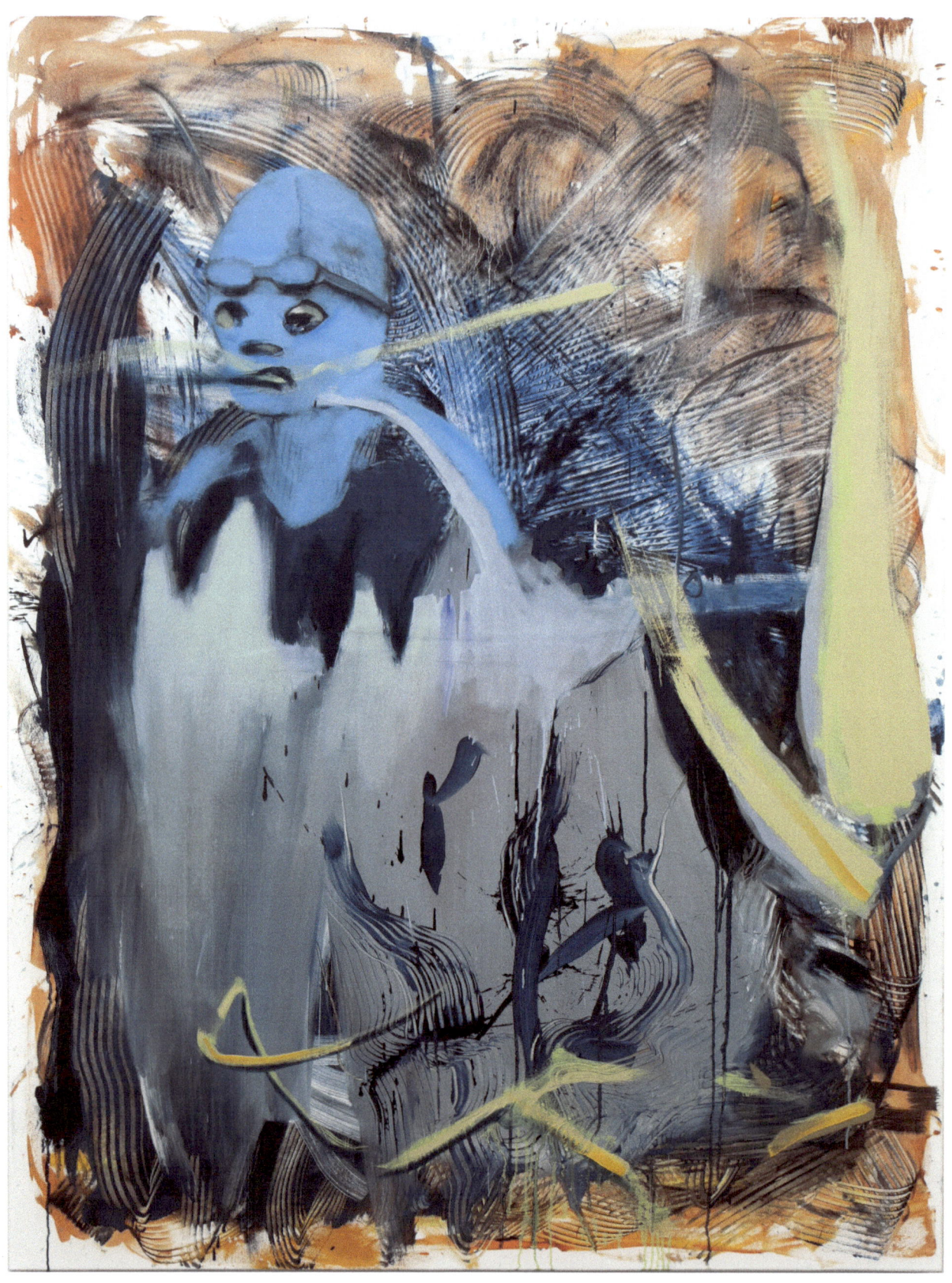

Blue Fellows III

oil on canvas

178x127cm

2014

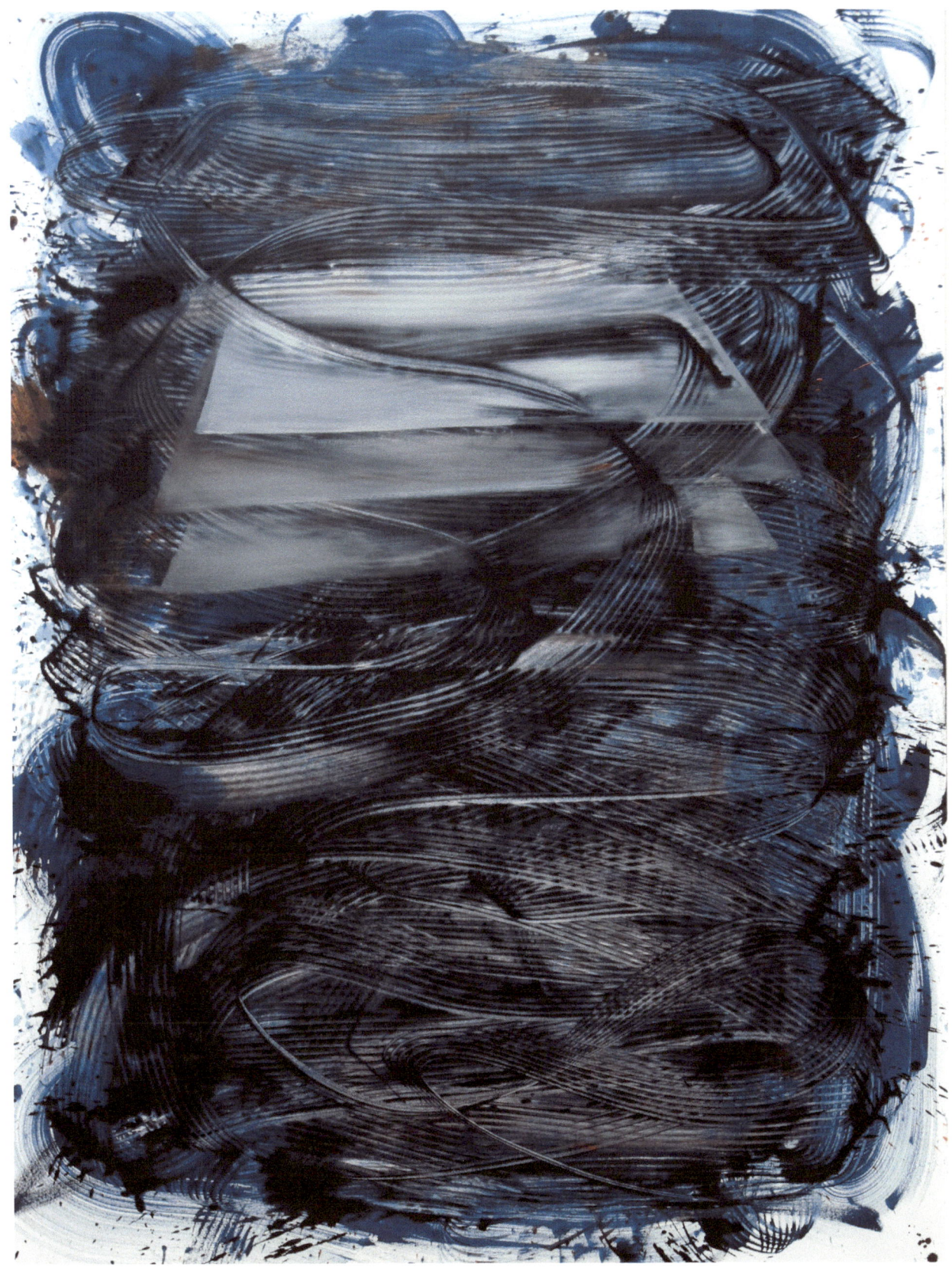

Blue Fellows

oil on canvas

183x147cm

2014

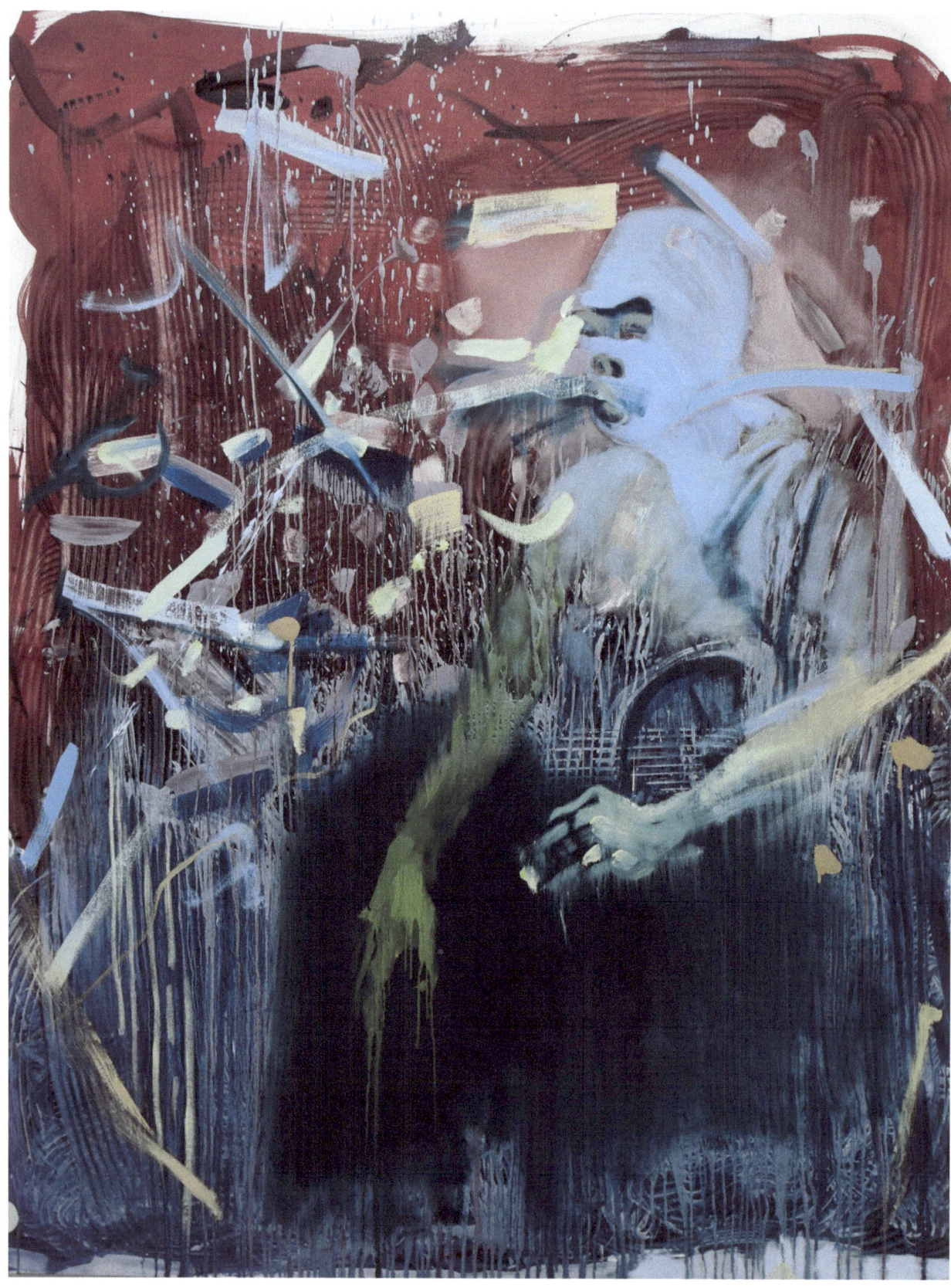

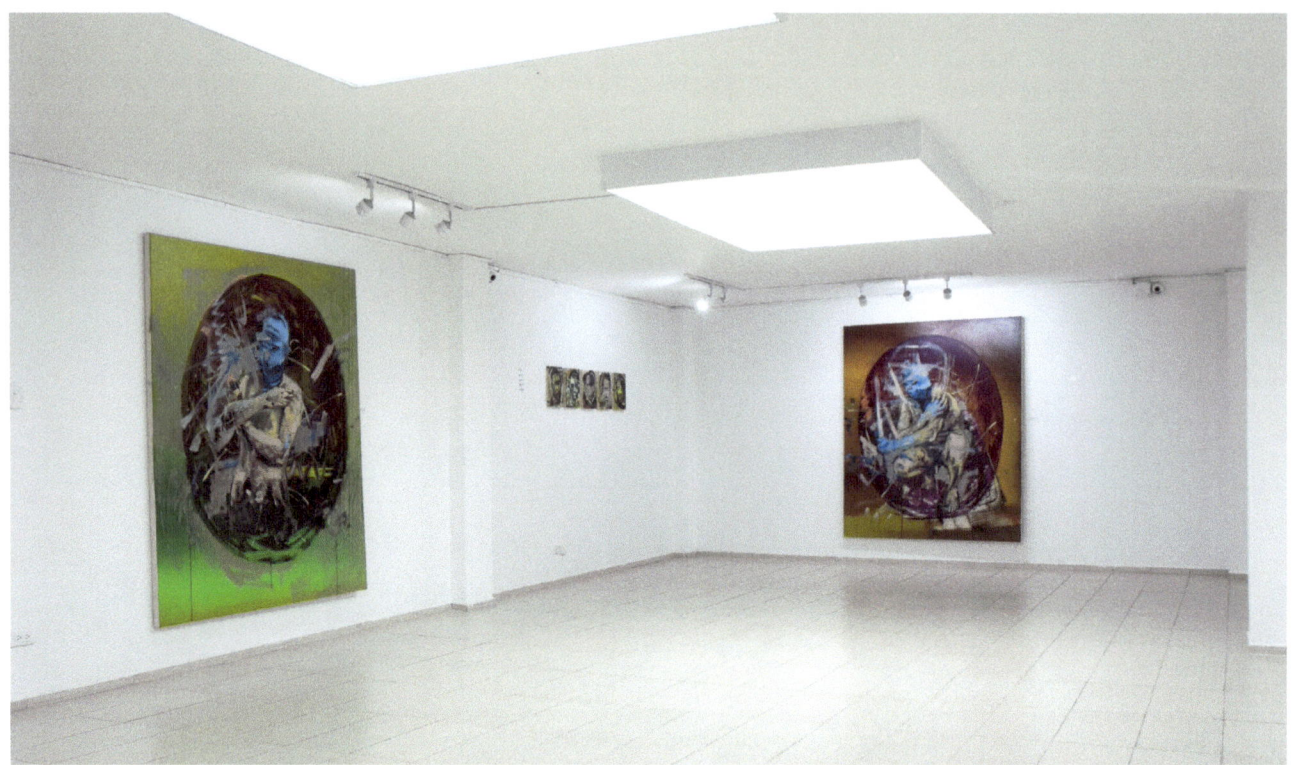

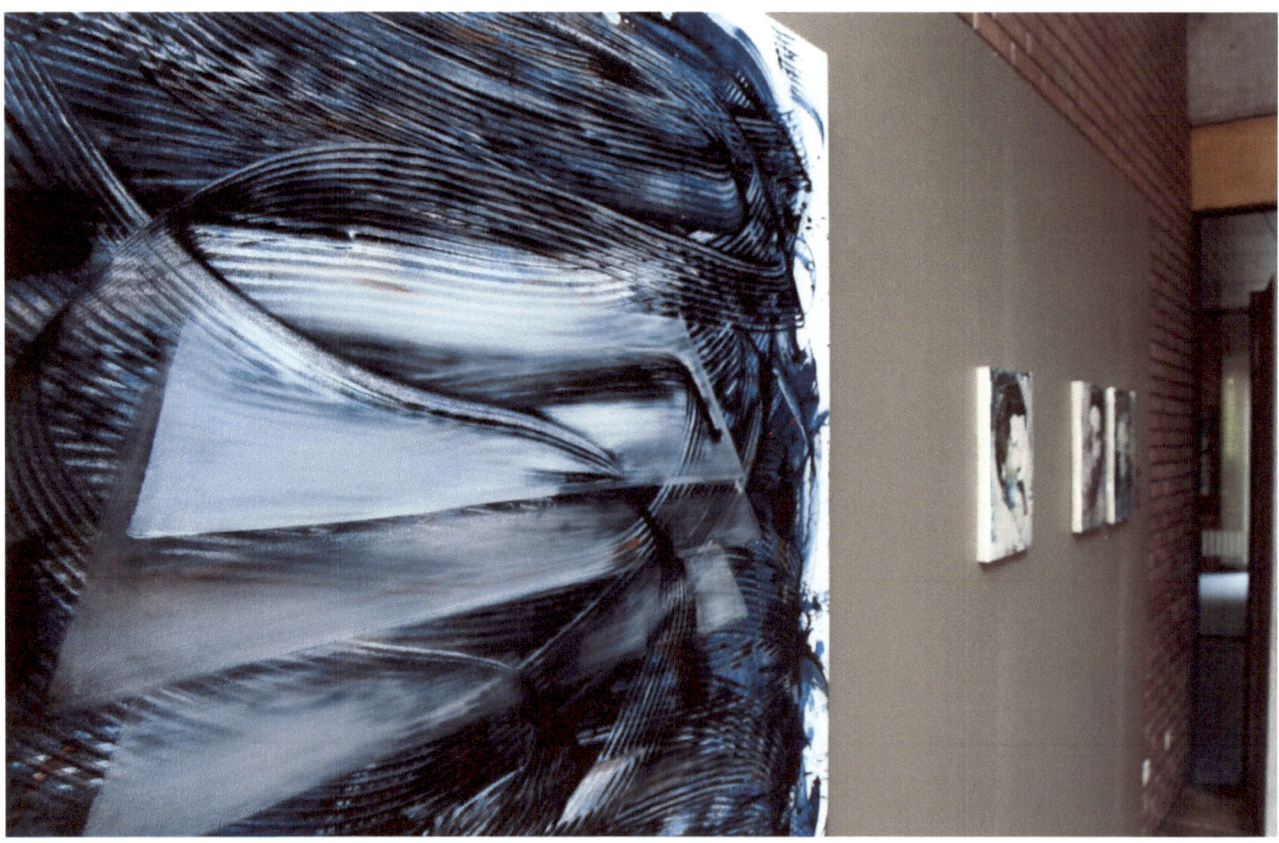

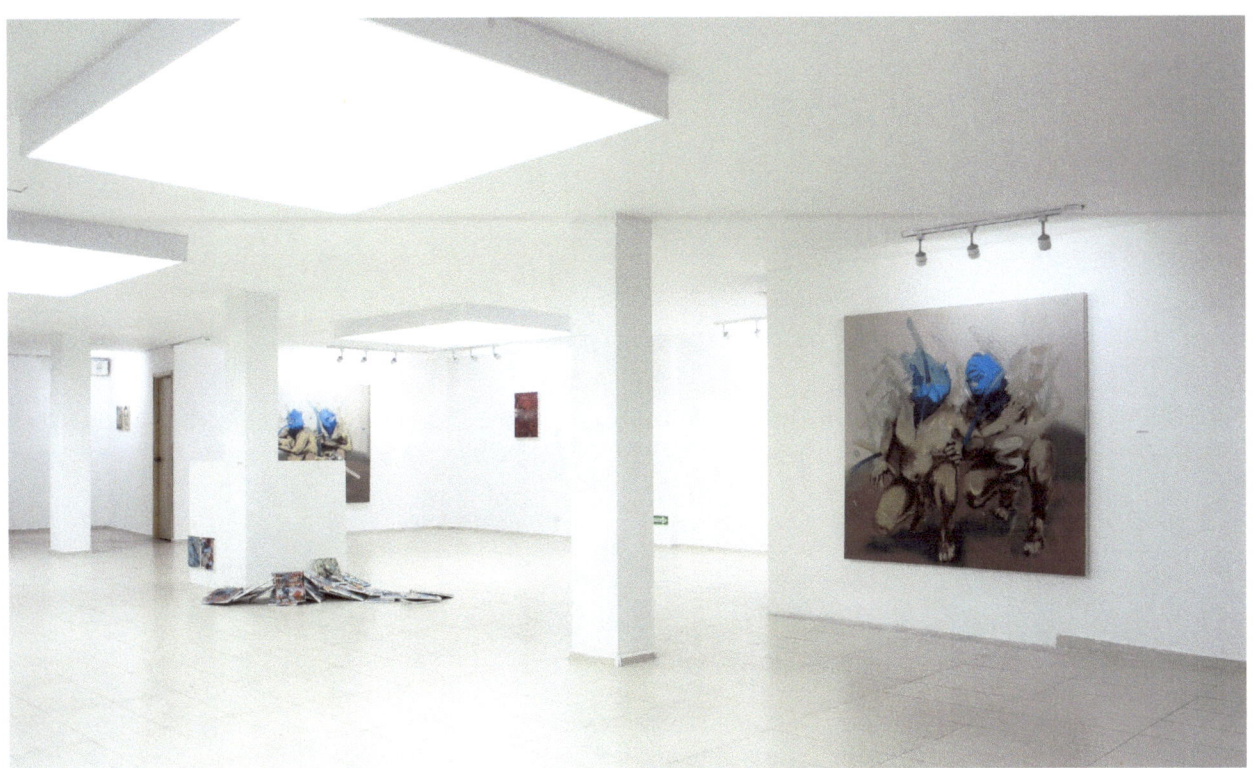

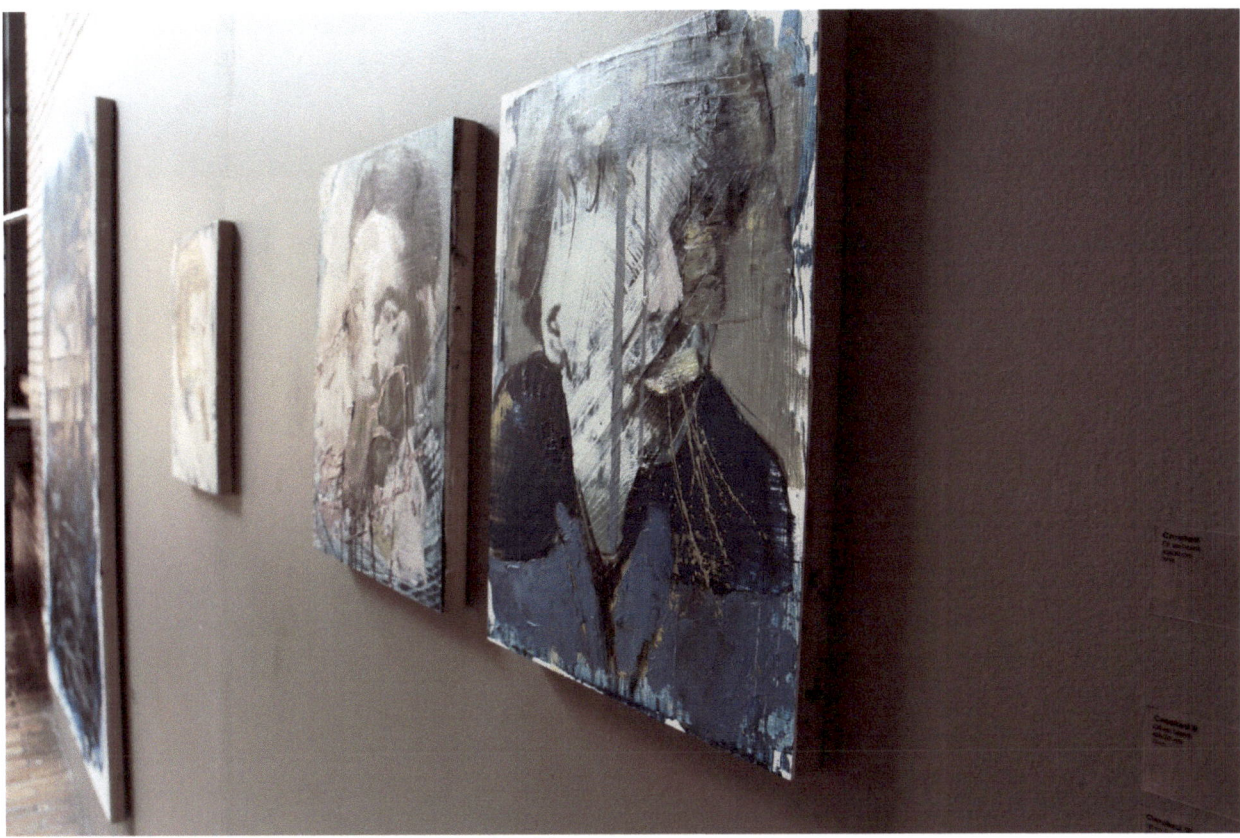

Solo Exhibitions

Bogota, Colombia

2014

Solaris II and III

oil on canvas

50x40cm

2014

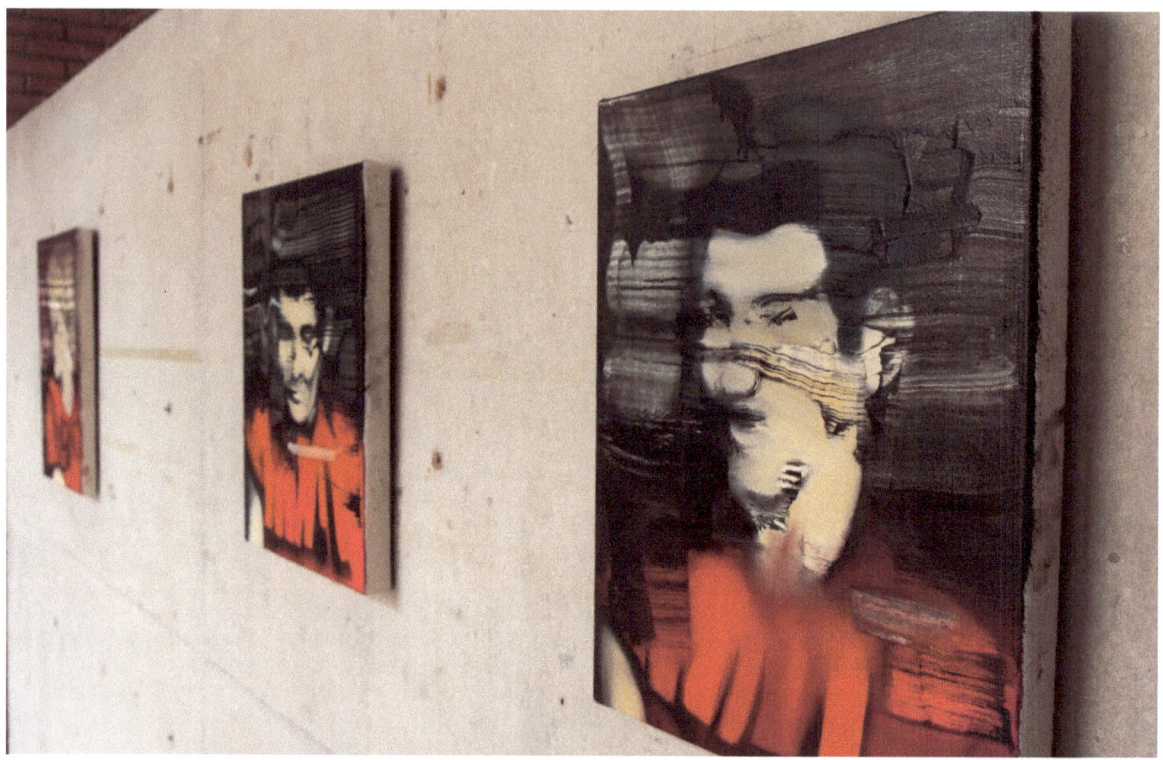

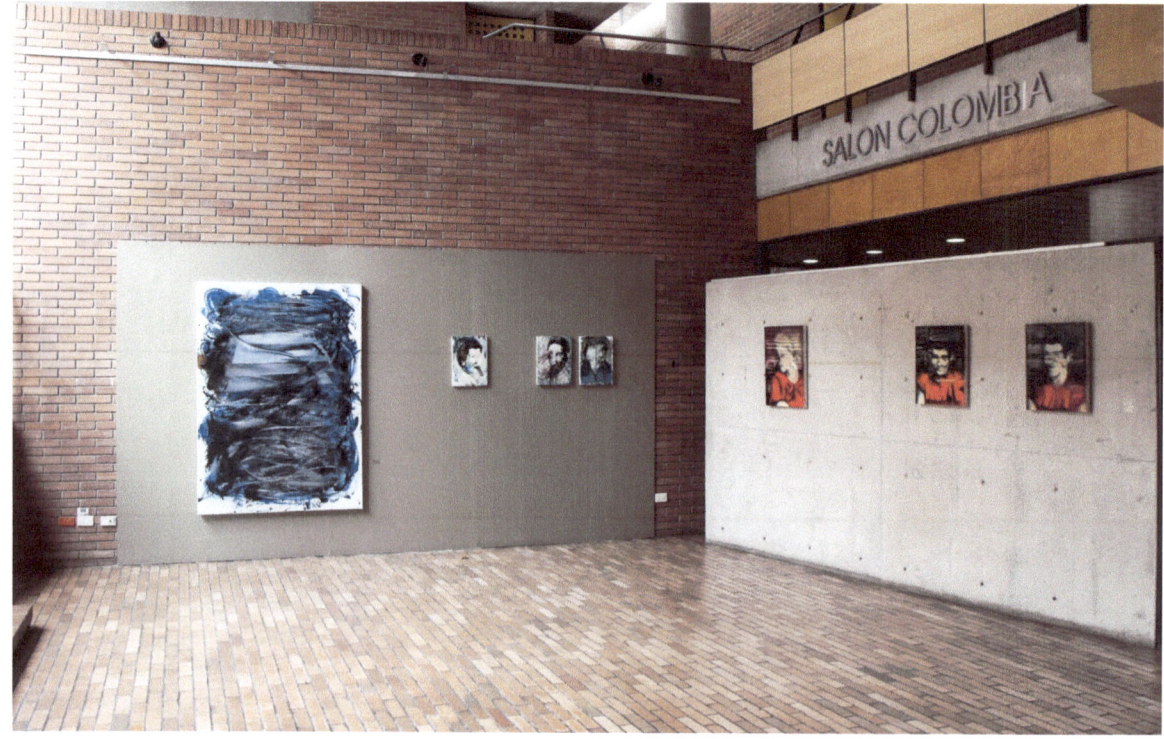

Solaris I

oil on canvas

59x41cm

2014

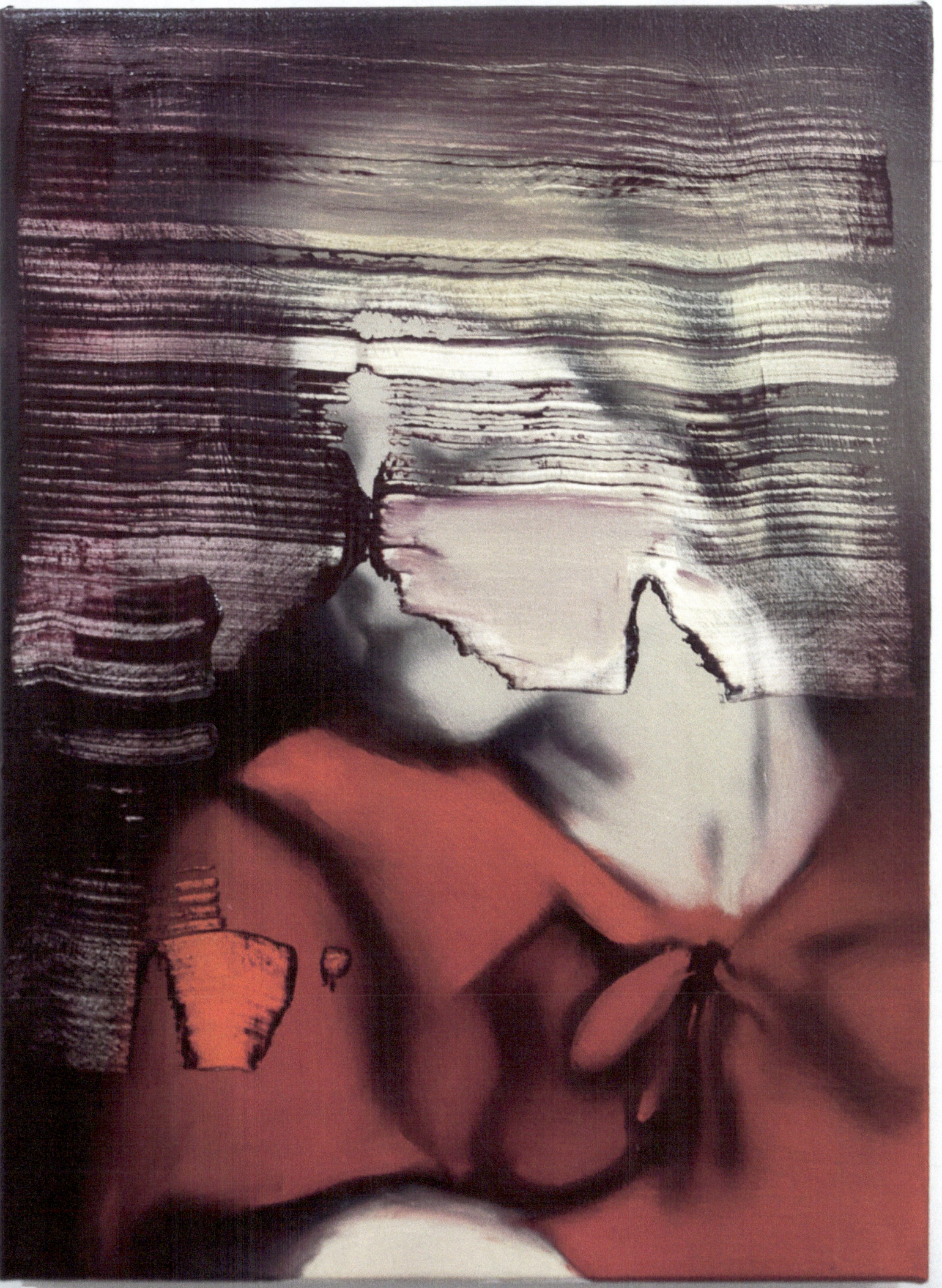

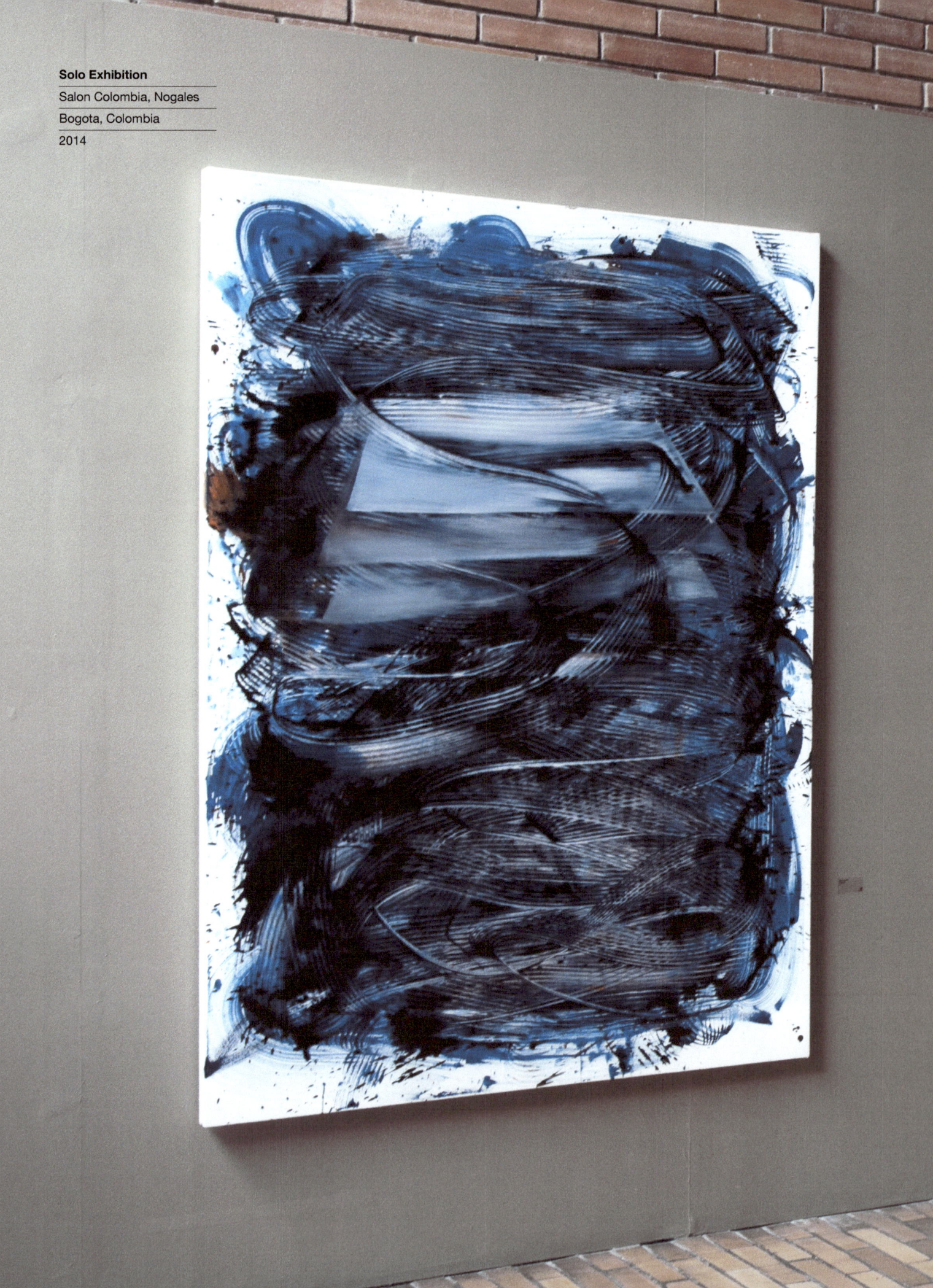

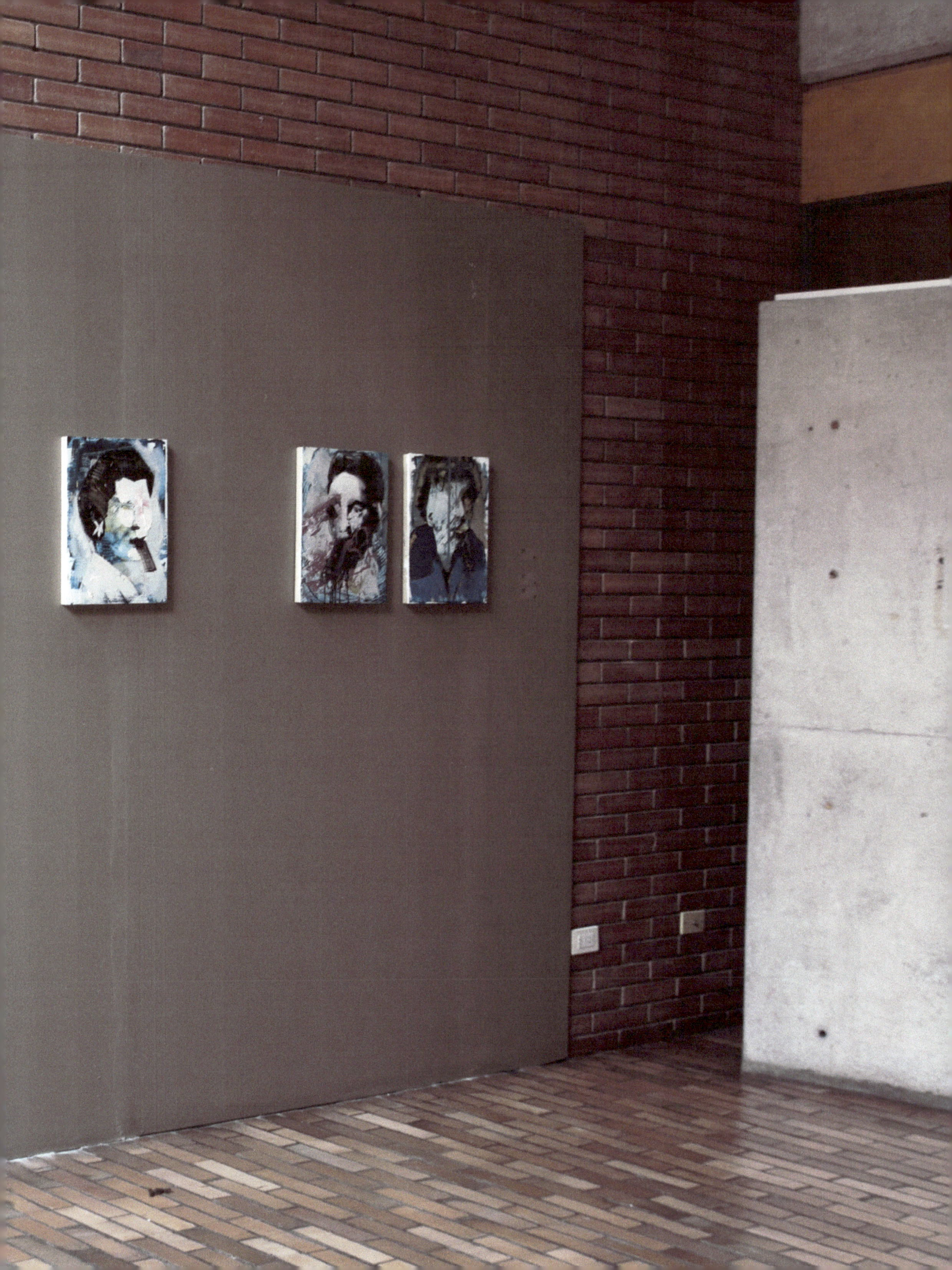

Extraordinarious

oil on canvas

183x153cm

2014

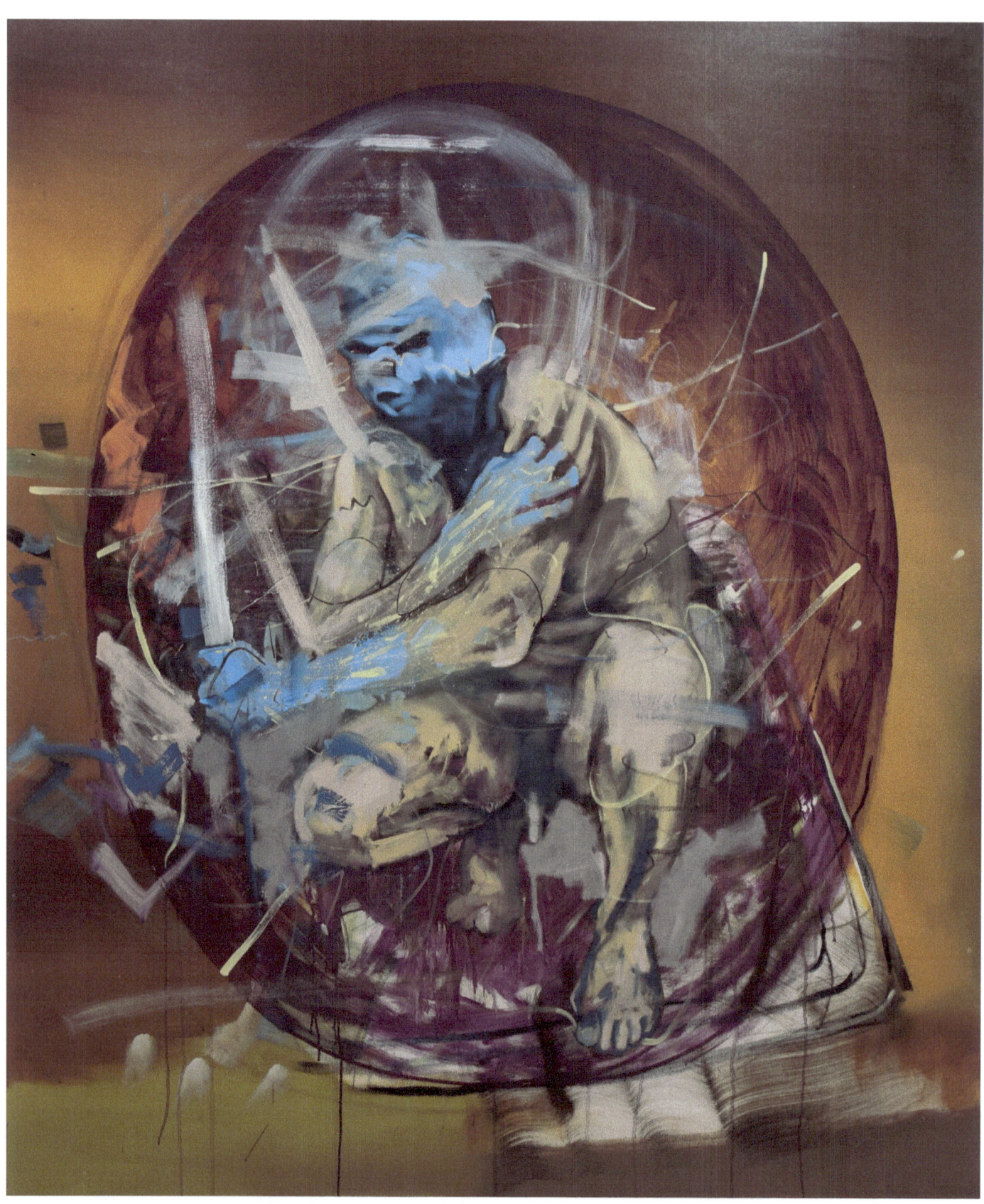

Extraordinarious II

oil on canvas

183x153cm

2014

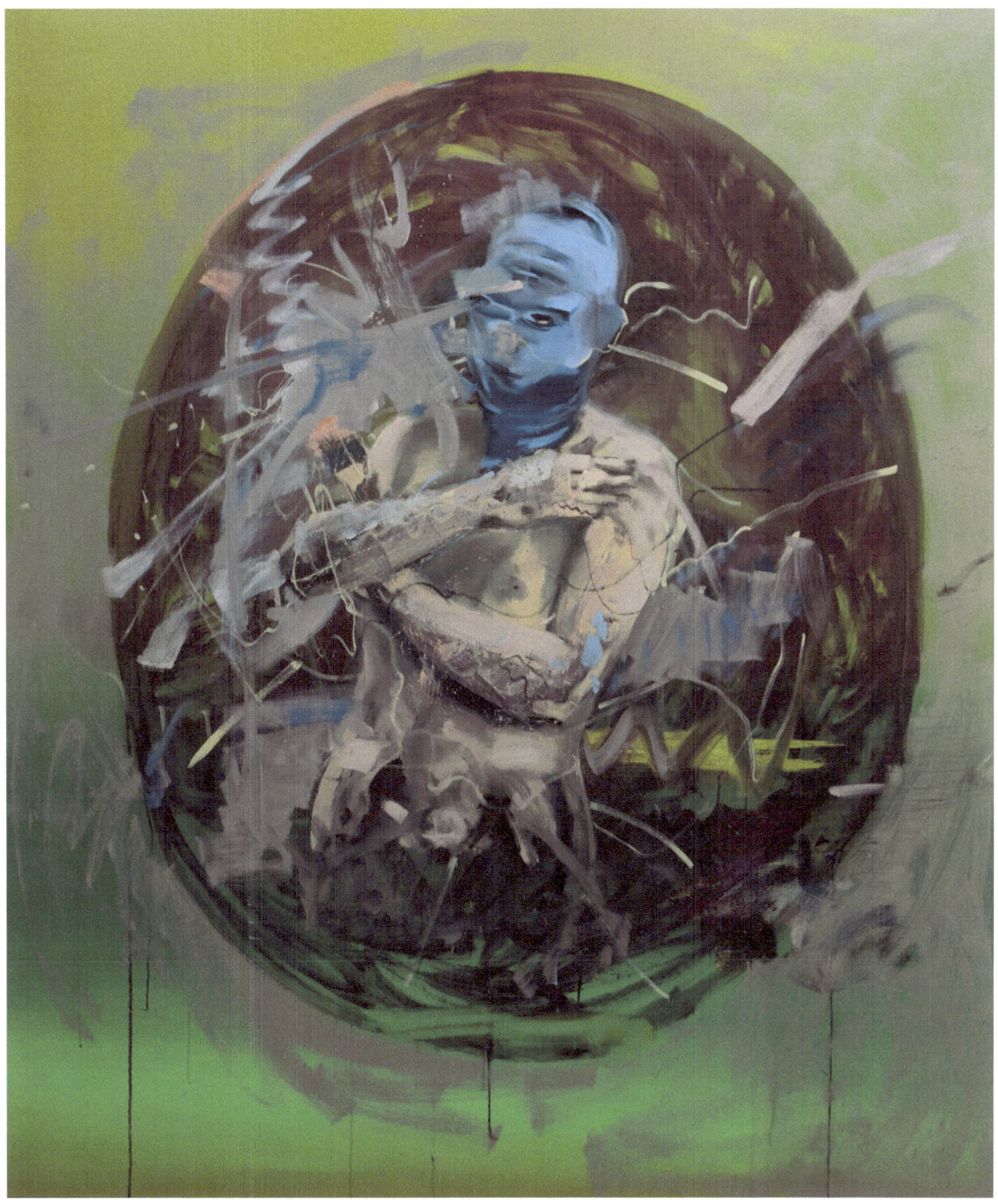

One Side Other Side I

oil on canvas

77x77cm

2014

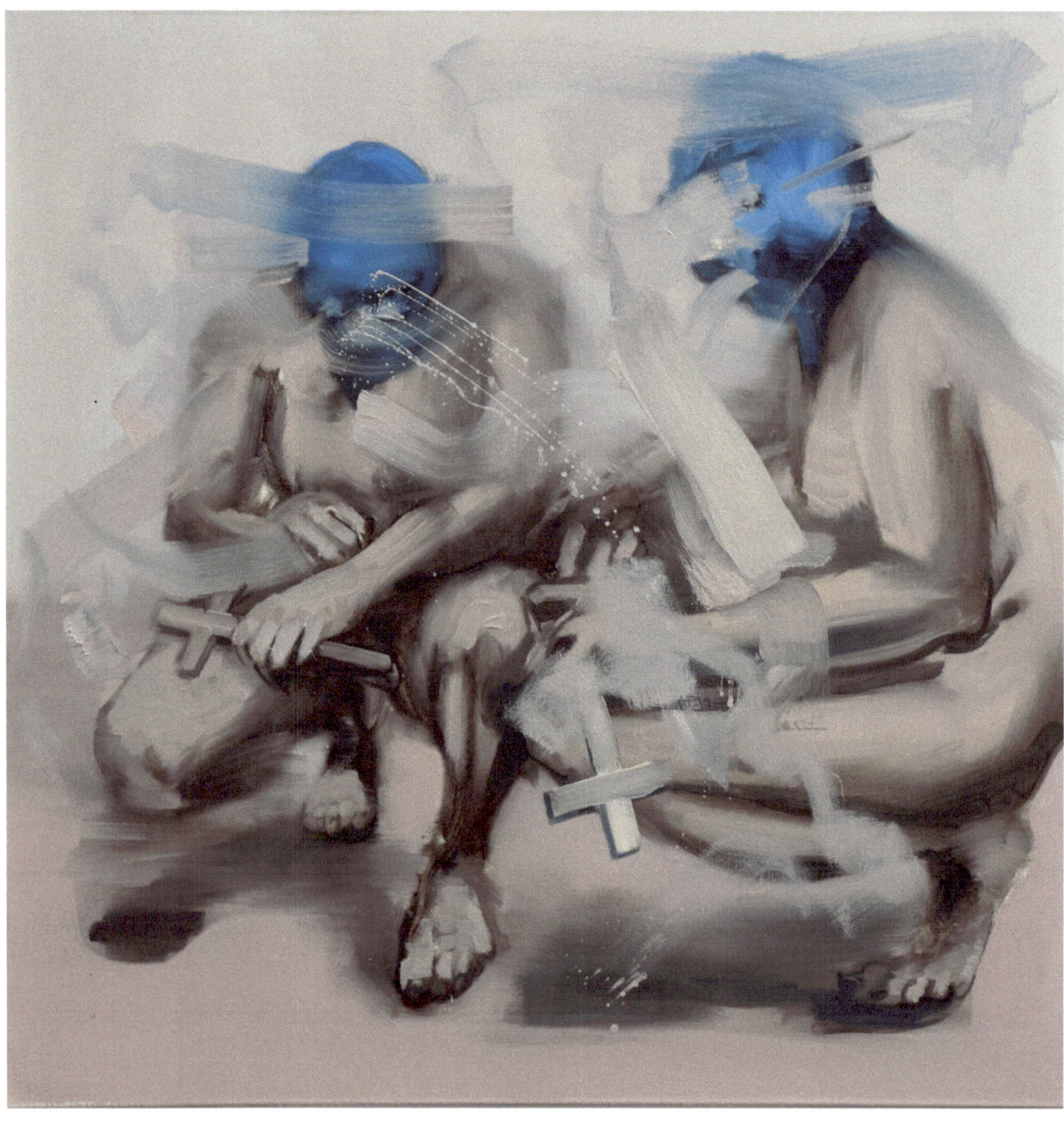

Othello II

oil on canvas

153x153cm

2014

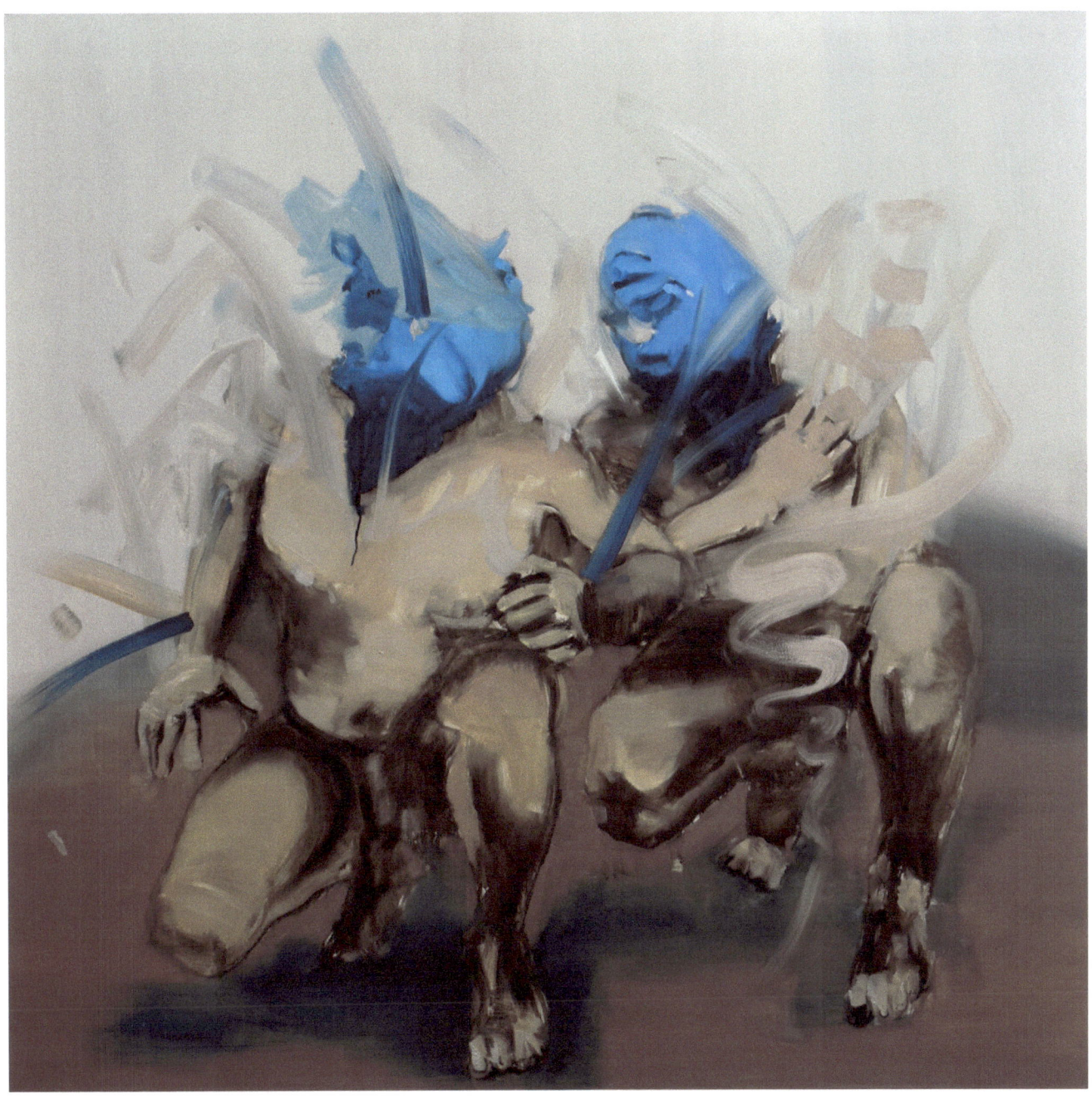

Temptation

oil on canvas

64x46cm

2014

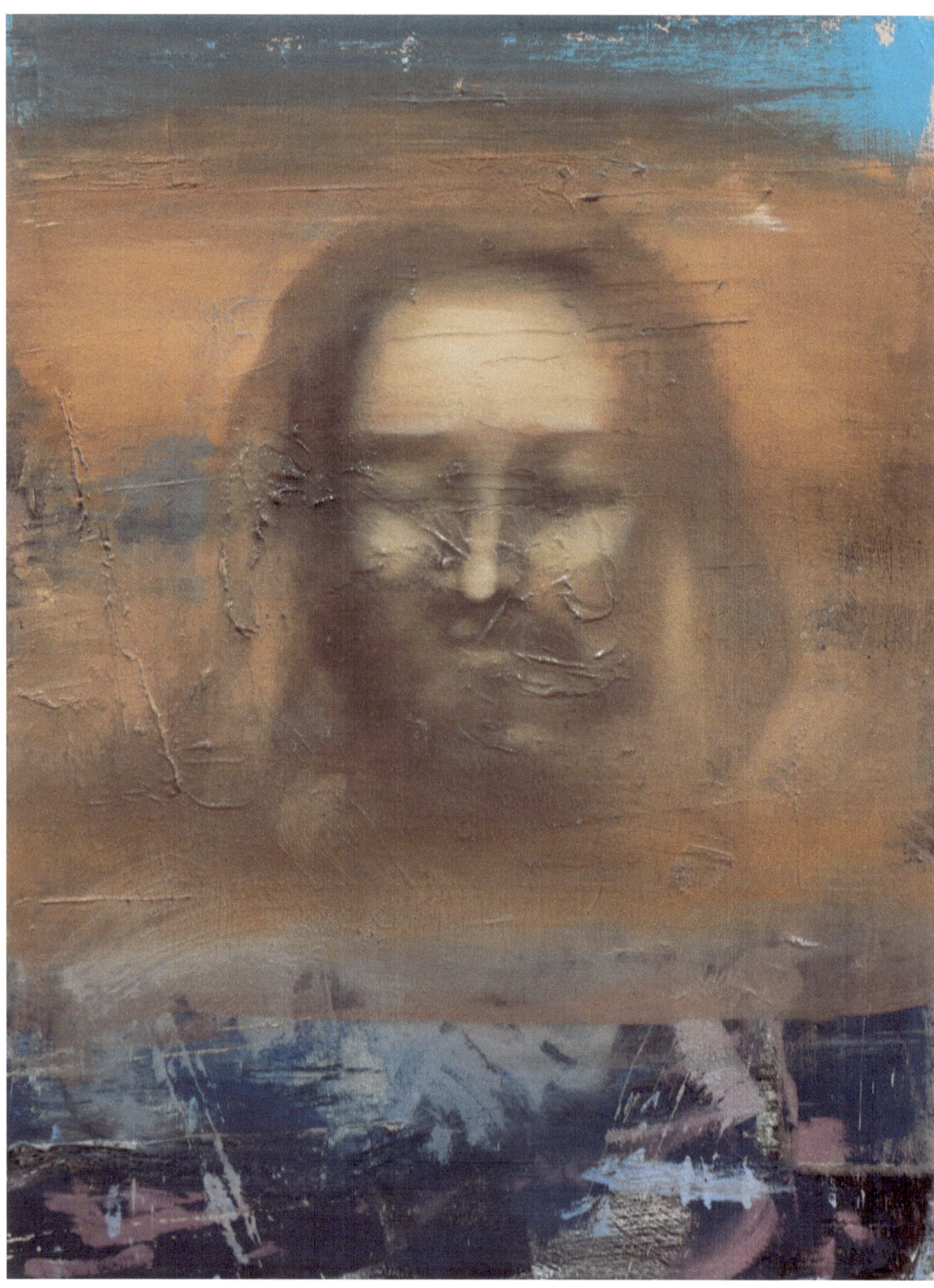

Tempation II

oil on canvas

64x46cm

2014

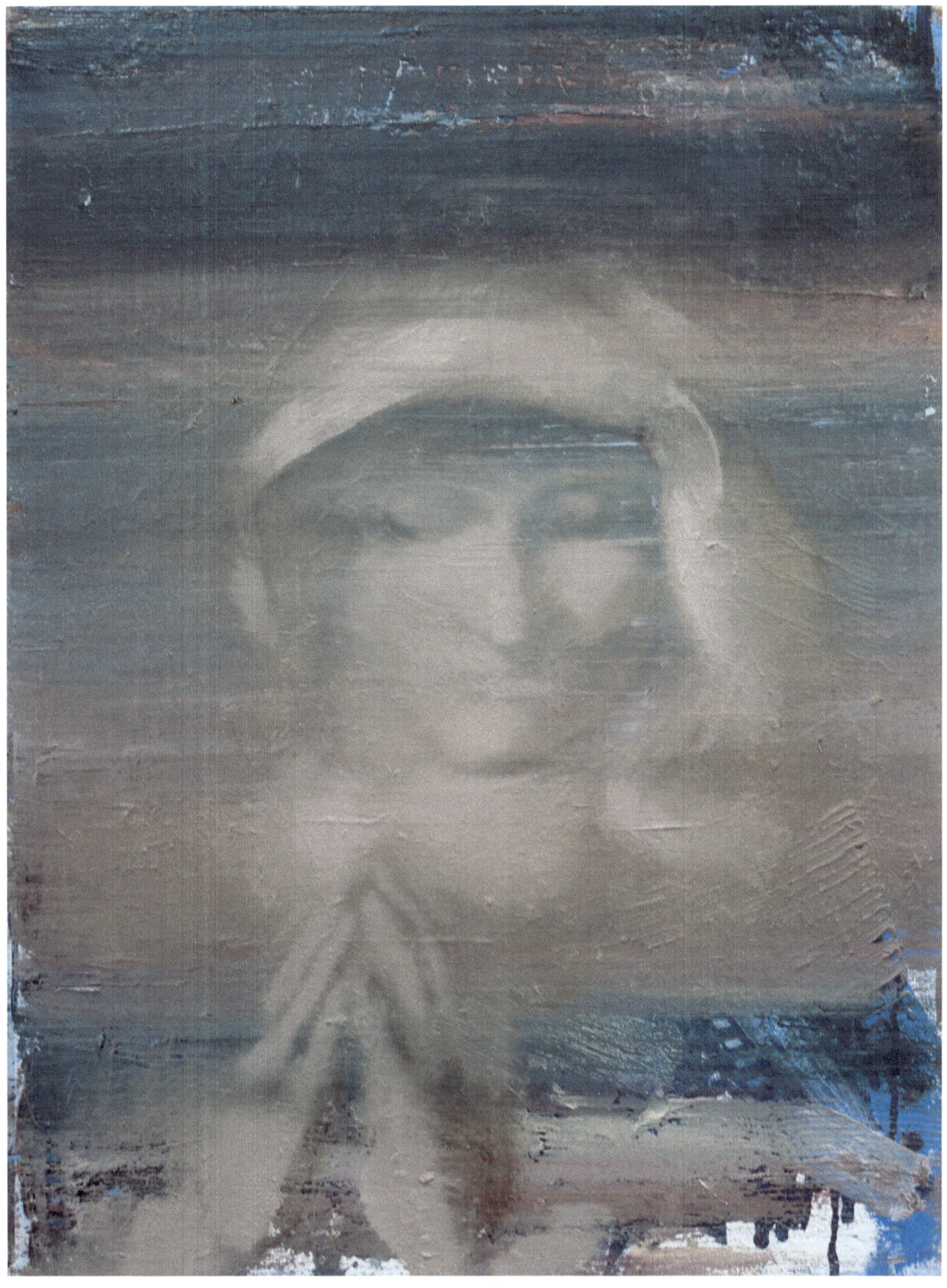

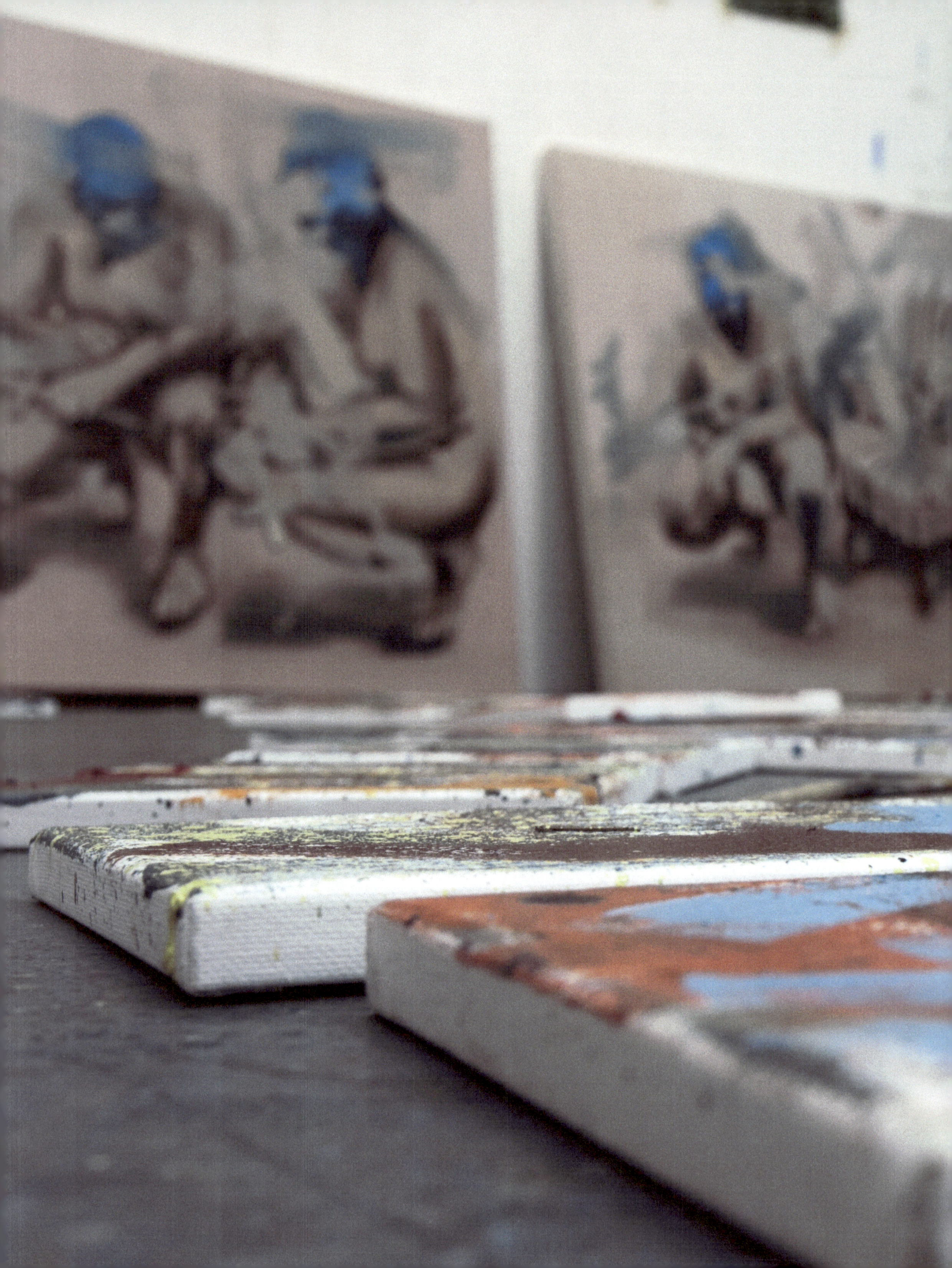

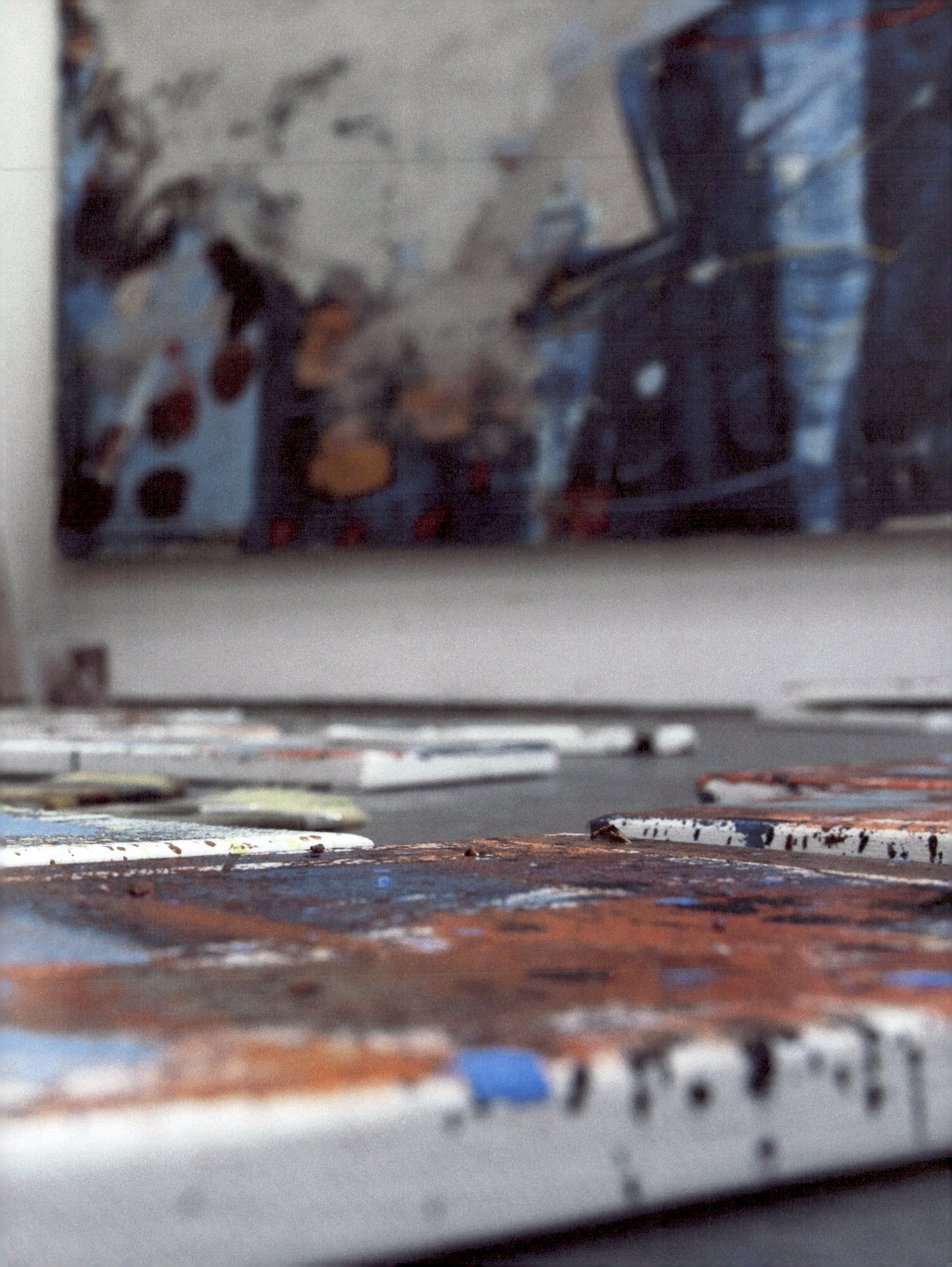

Seduction Series

Seduction I

oil on canvas

50x41cm

2014

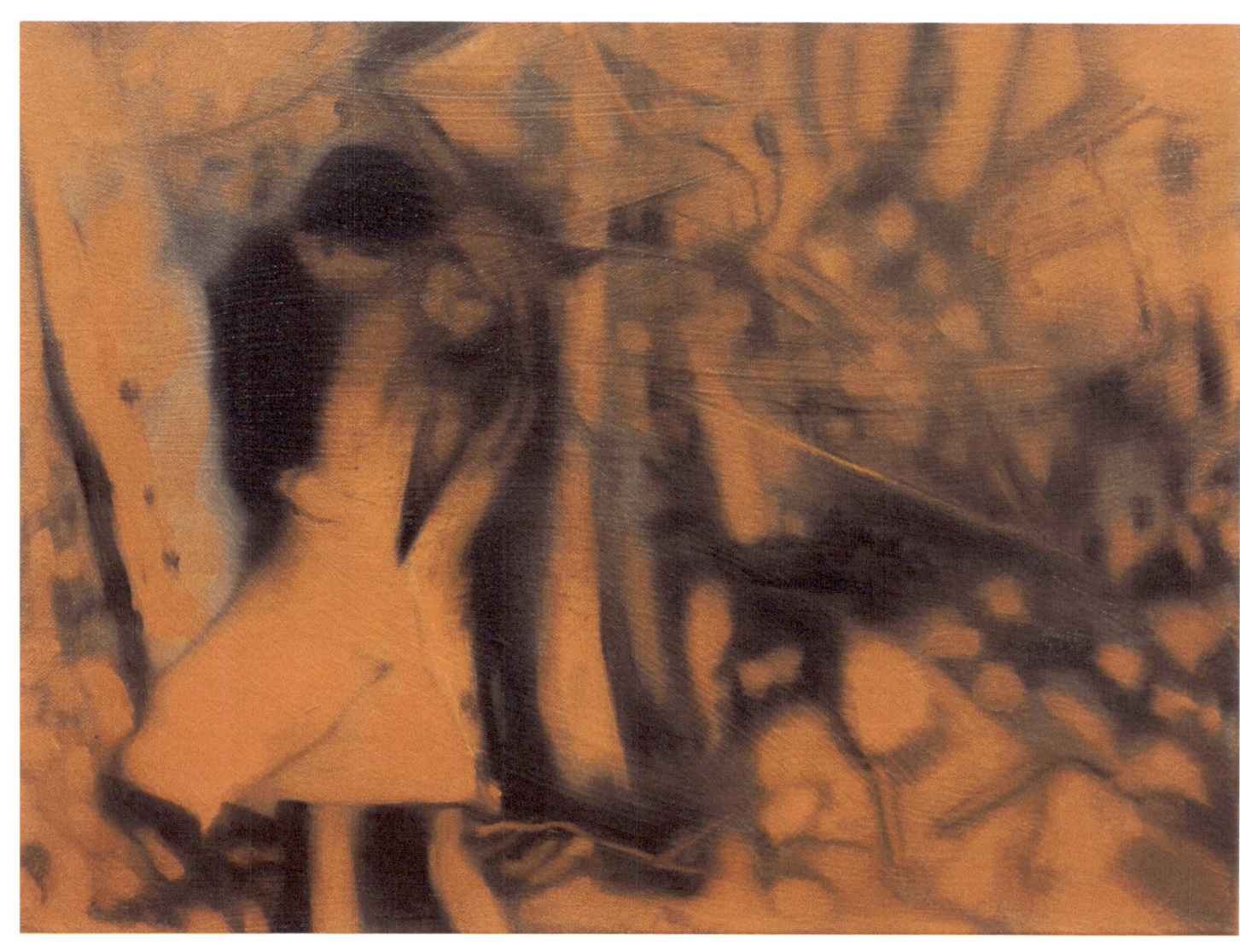

Seduction II

oil on canvas

50x41cm

2014

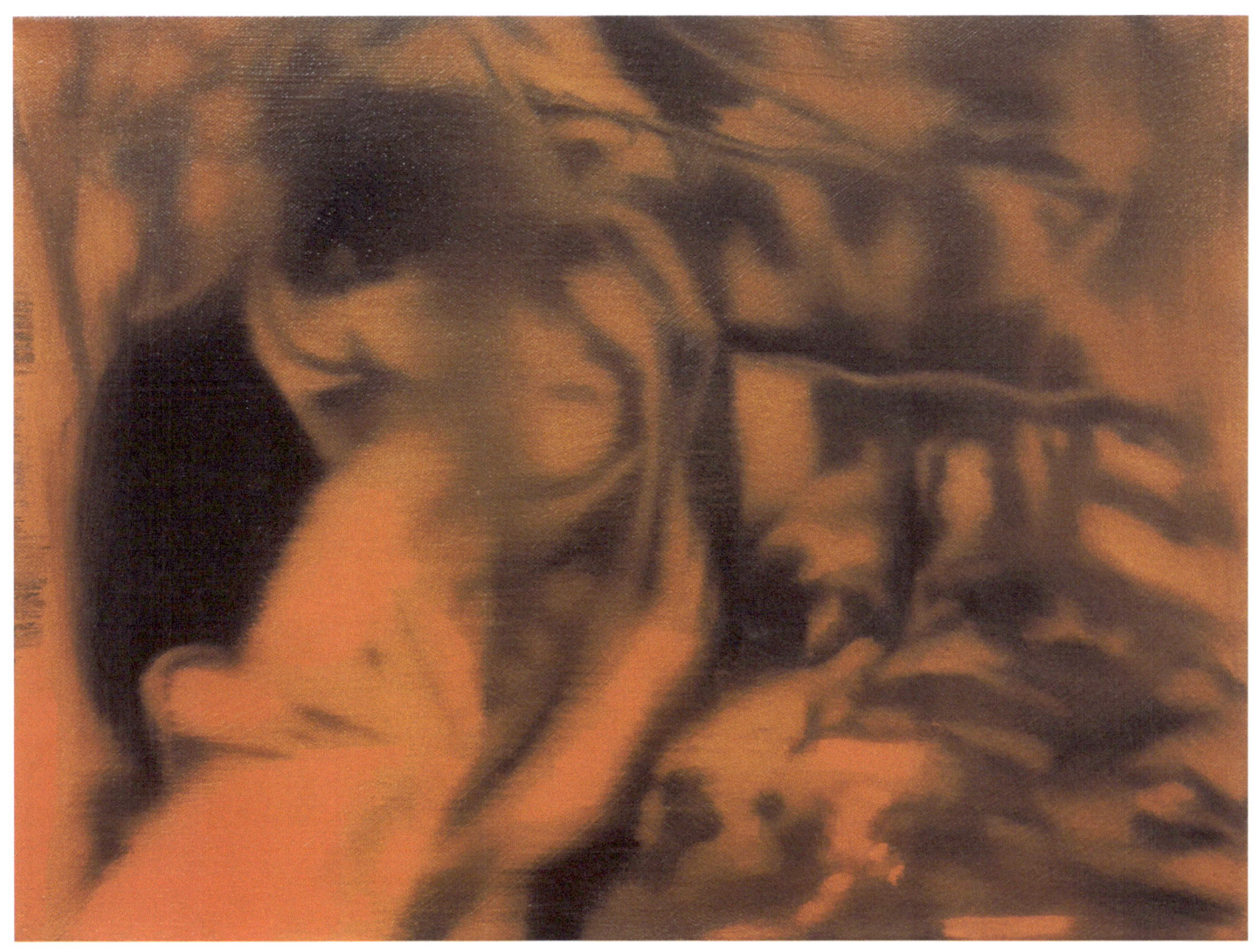

Seduction III

oil on canvas

50x41cm

2014

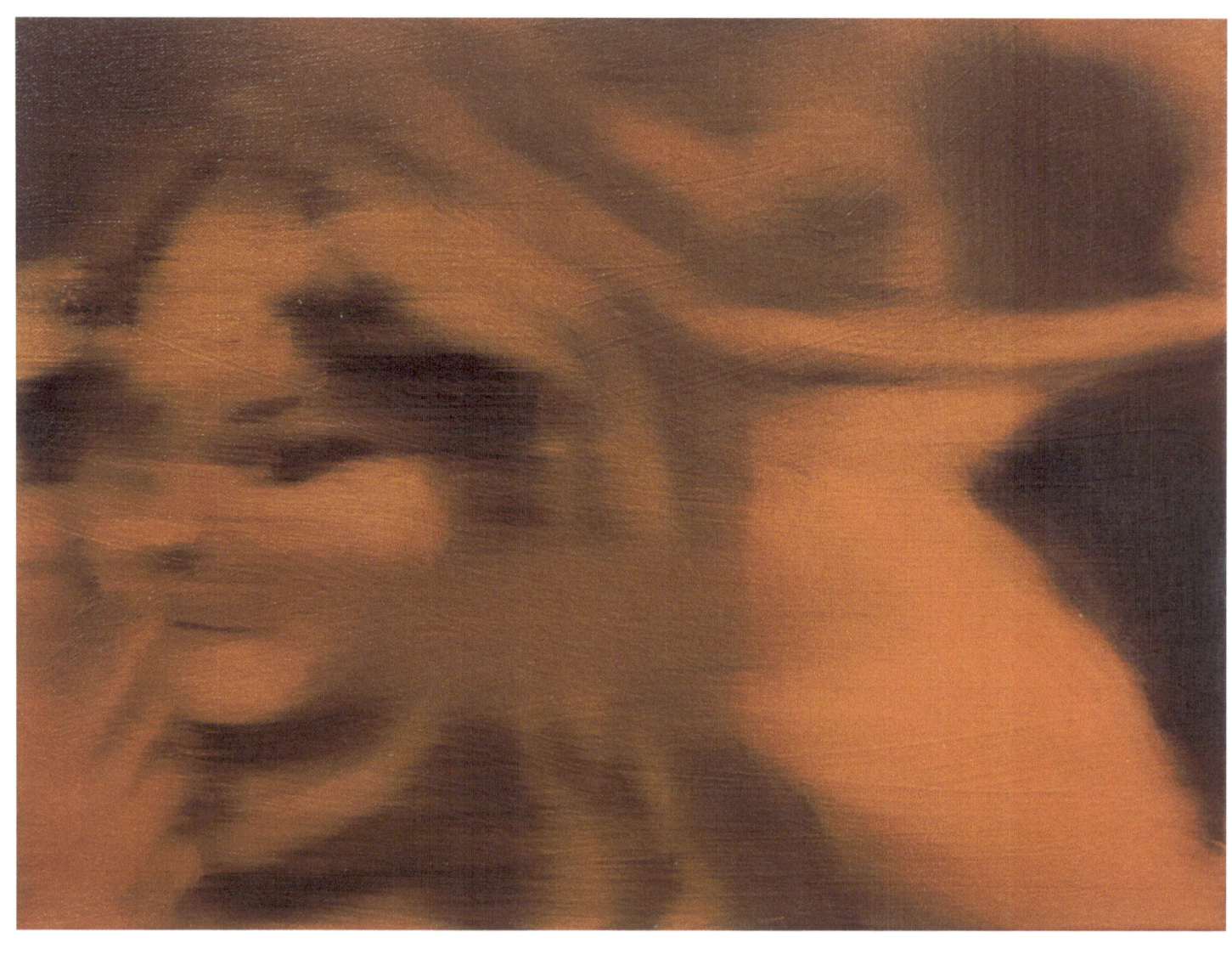

I paint every day. However at this point in my career it is too early for me to definitively answer the question, "What is painting?" Mark Rothko was asked how long it takes him to paint one painting. He replied "my whole life." This may sound like a joke or cocky reply, but if we think about it more, his answer was appropriate. In order to understand what painting is, we must realize it is much more than a definition. Sometimes it takes a whole life to understand.

—Bartosz Beda

Repressed Wishes I

oil on canvas

46x38cm

2014

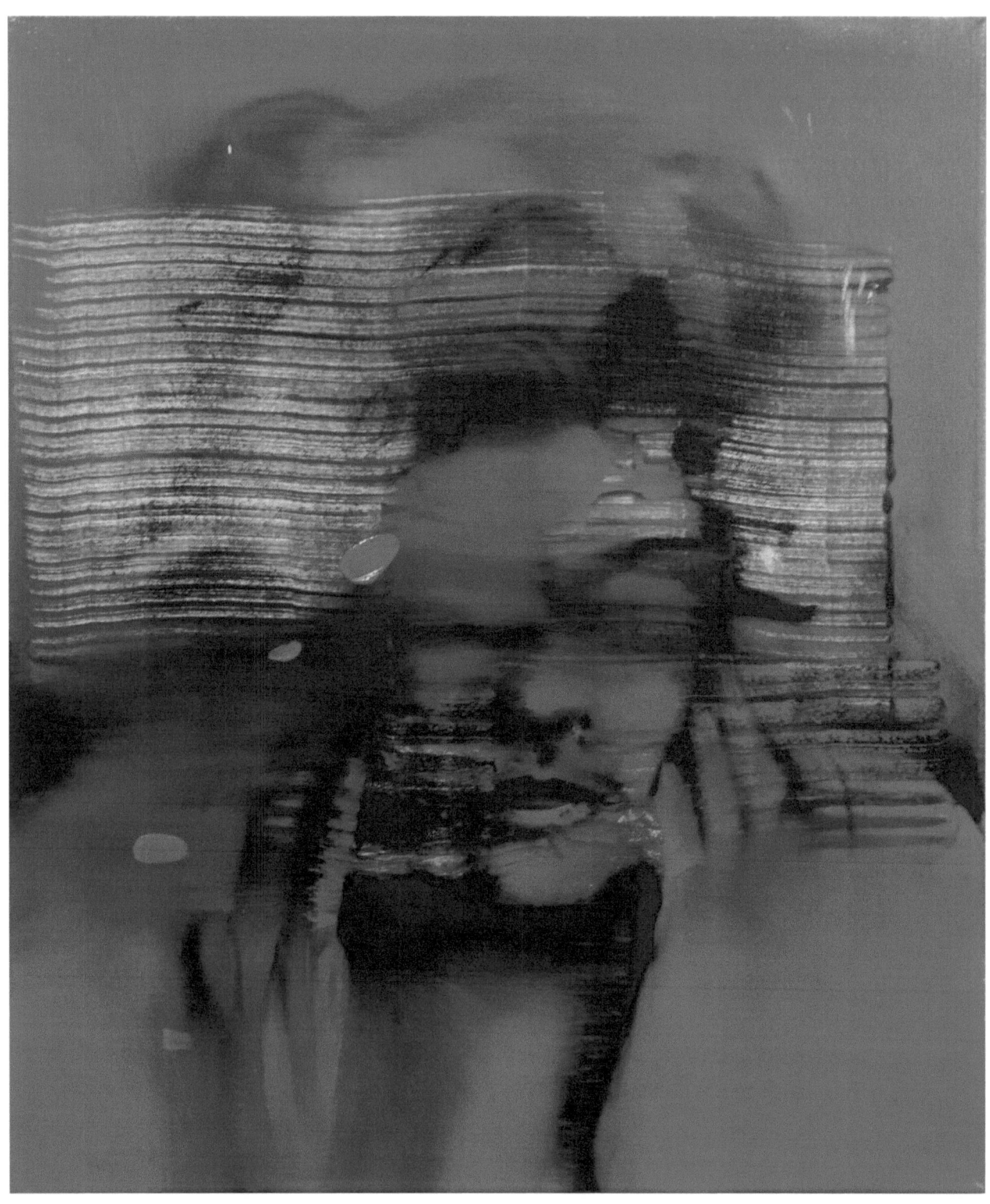

Repressed Wishes II

oil on canvas

46x38cm

2014

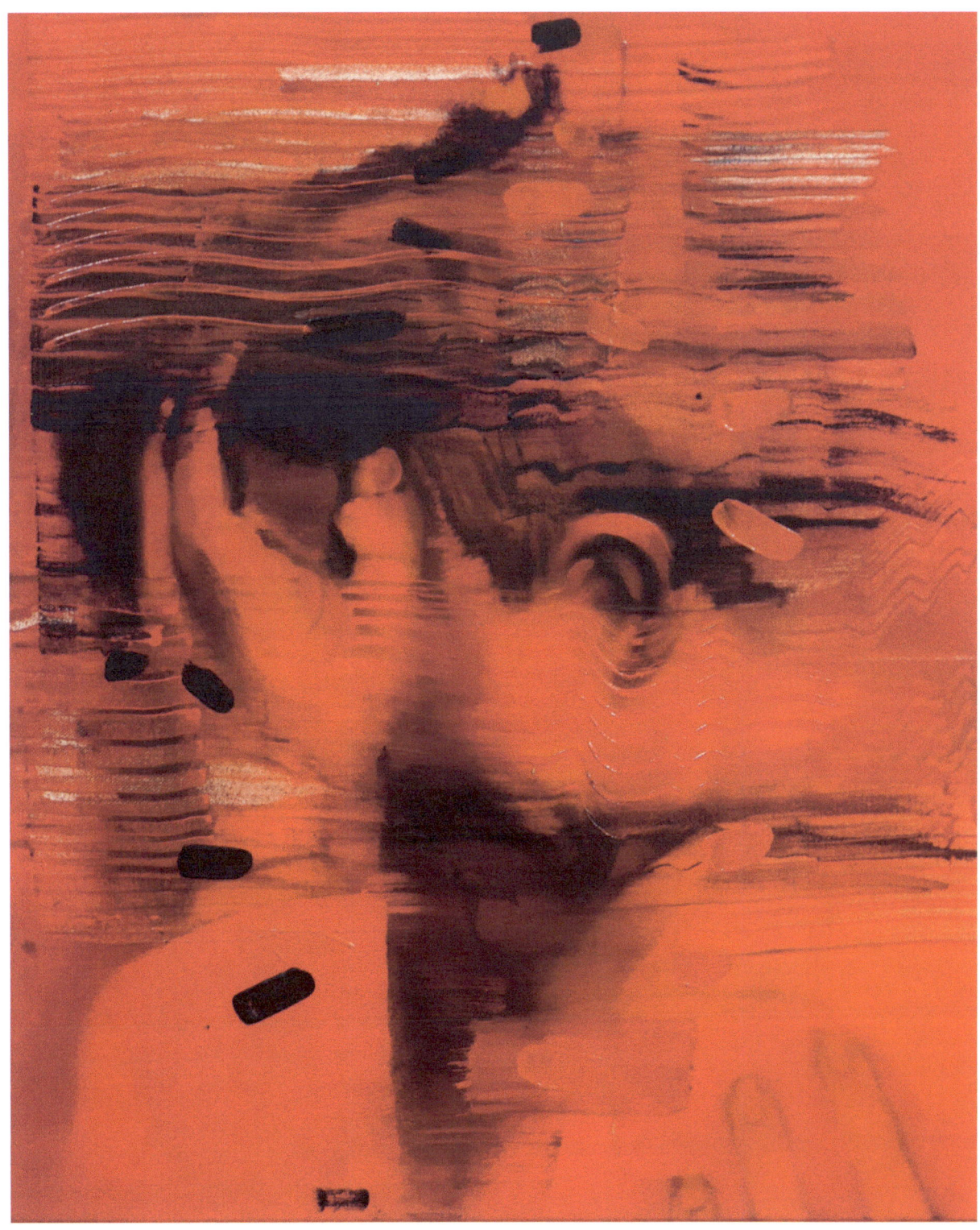

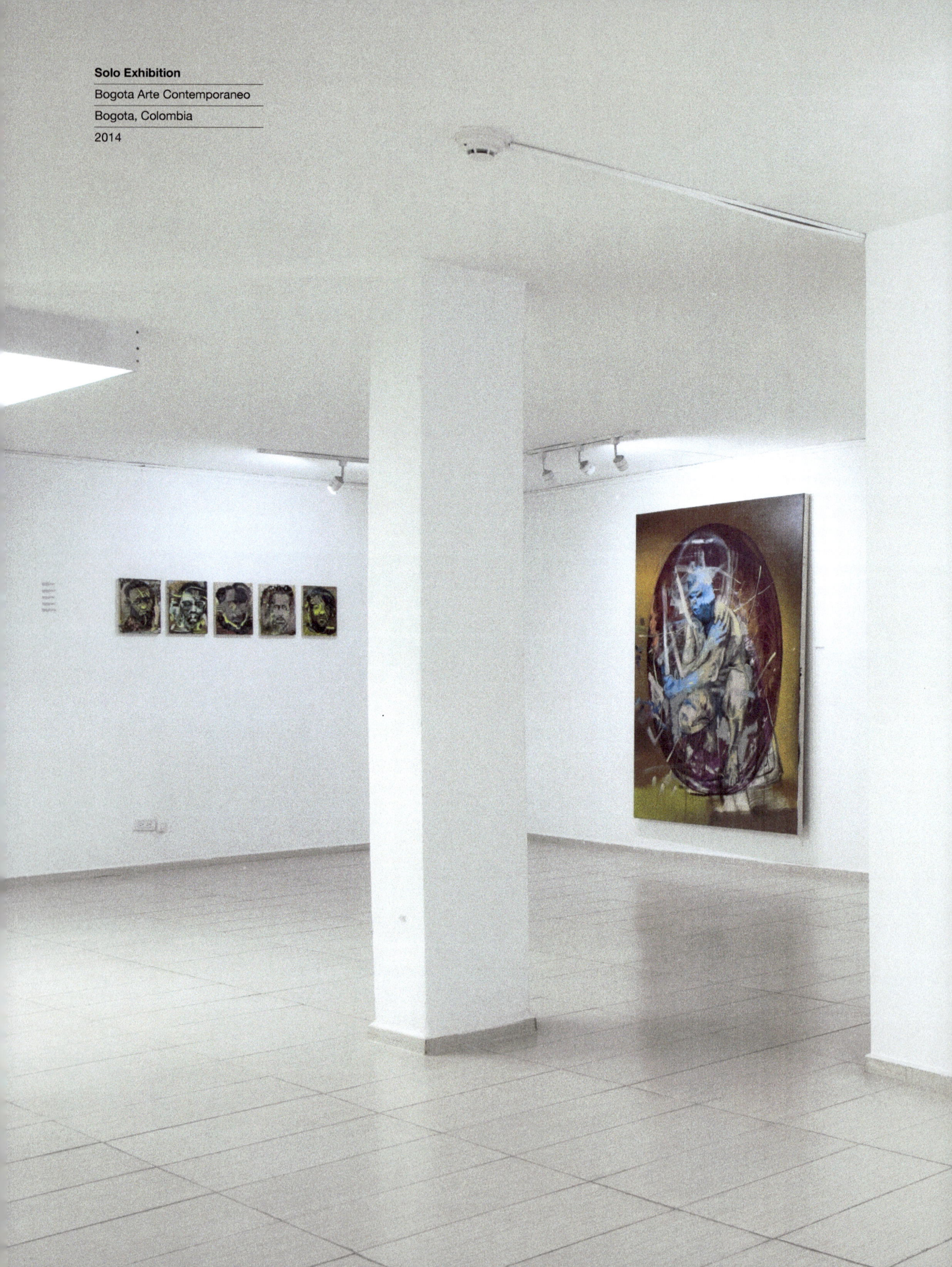

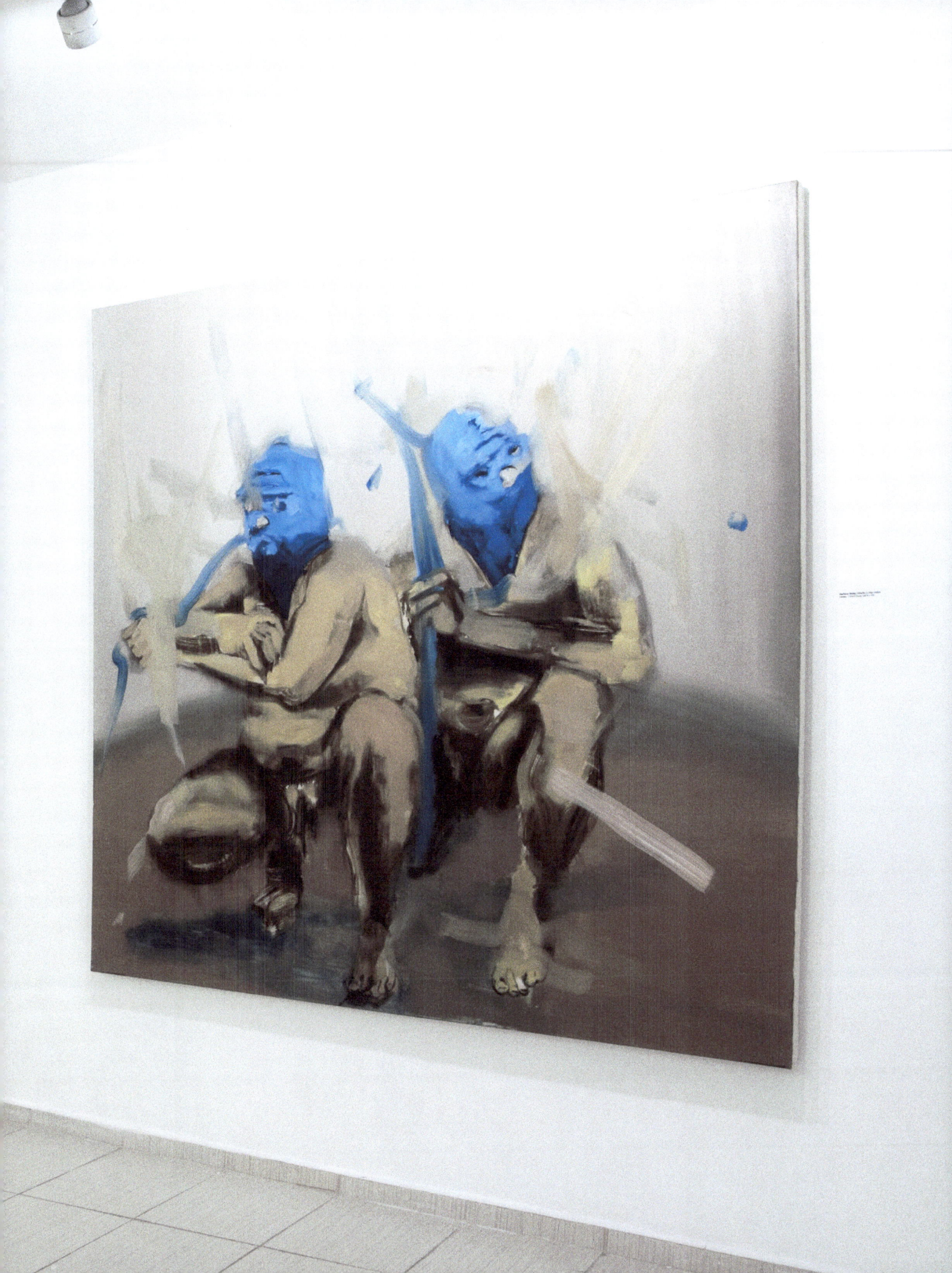

Looking at things Series

**Looking at things and
feeling good about them I**

oil on canvas

130x84cm

2015

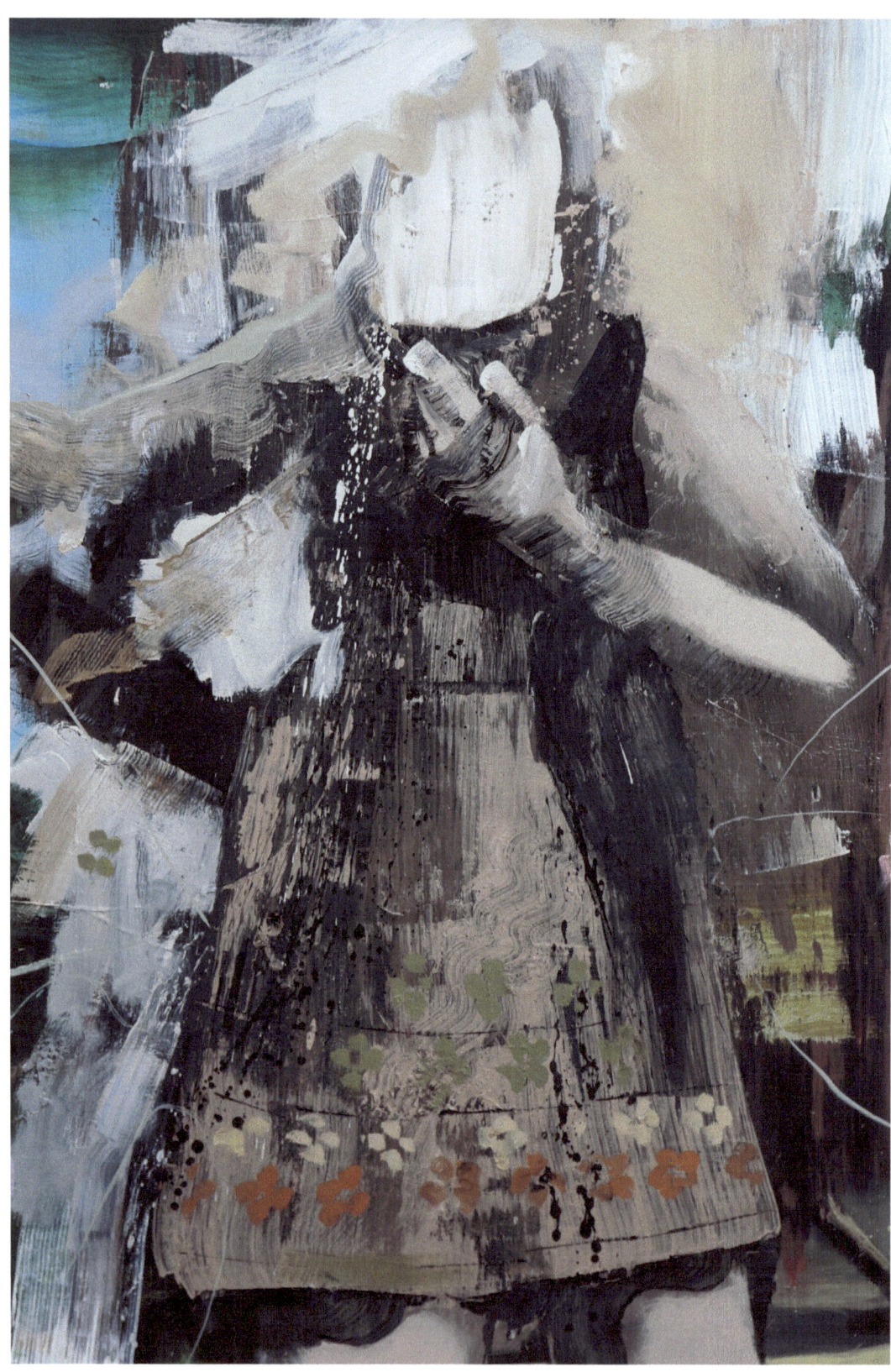

**Looking at things and
feeling good about them II**

oil on canvas

130x84cm

2015

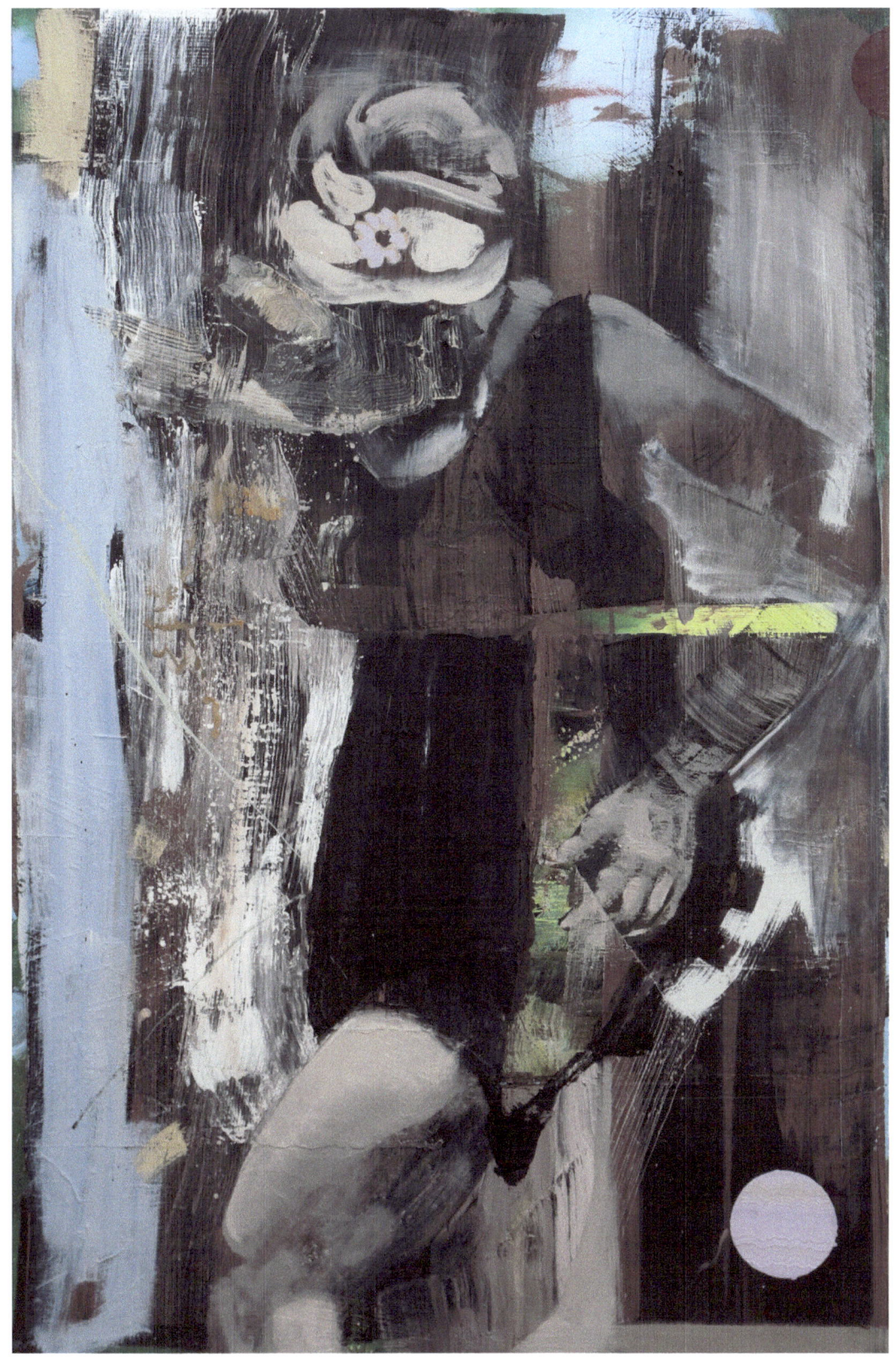

**Looking at things and
feeling good about them III**

oil on canvas

153x153cm

2015

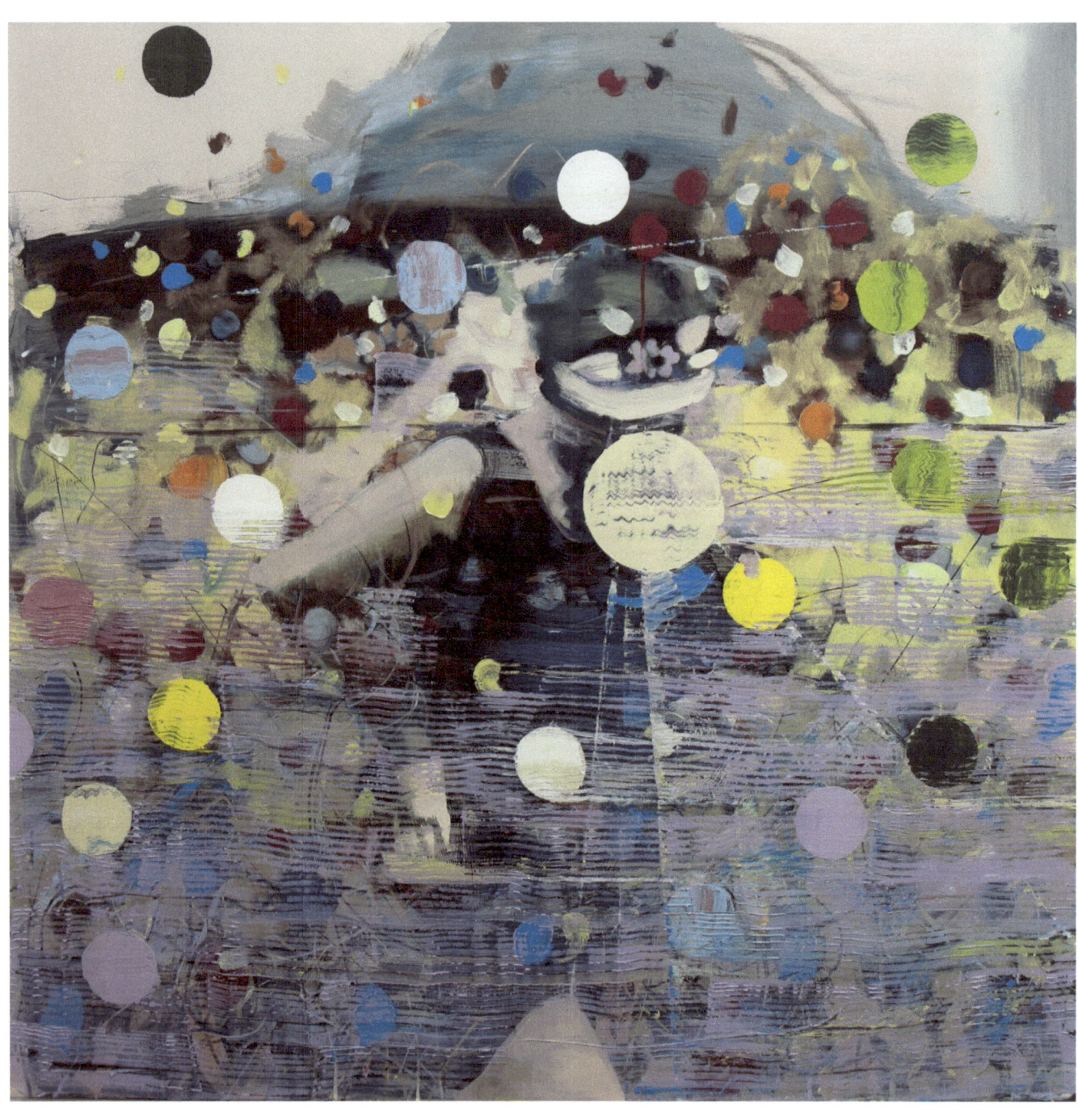

**Looking at things and
feeling good about them IV**

oil on canvas

132x102cm

2015

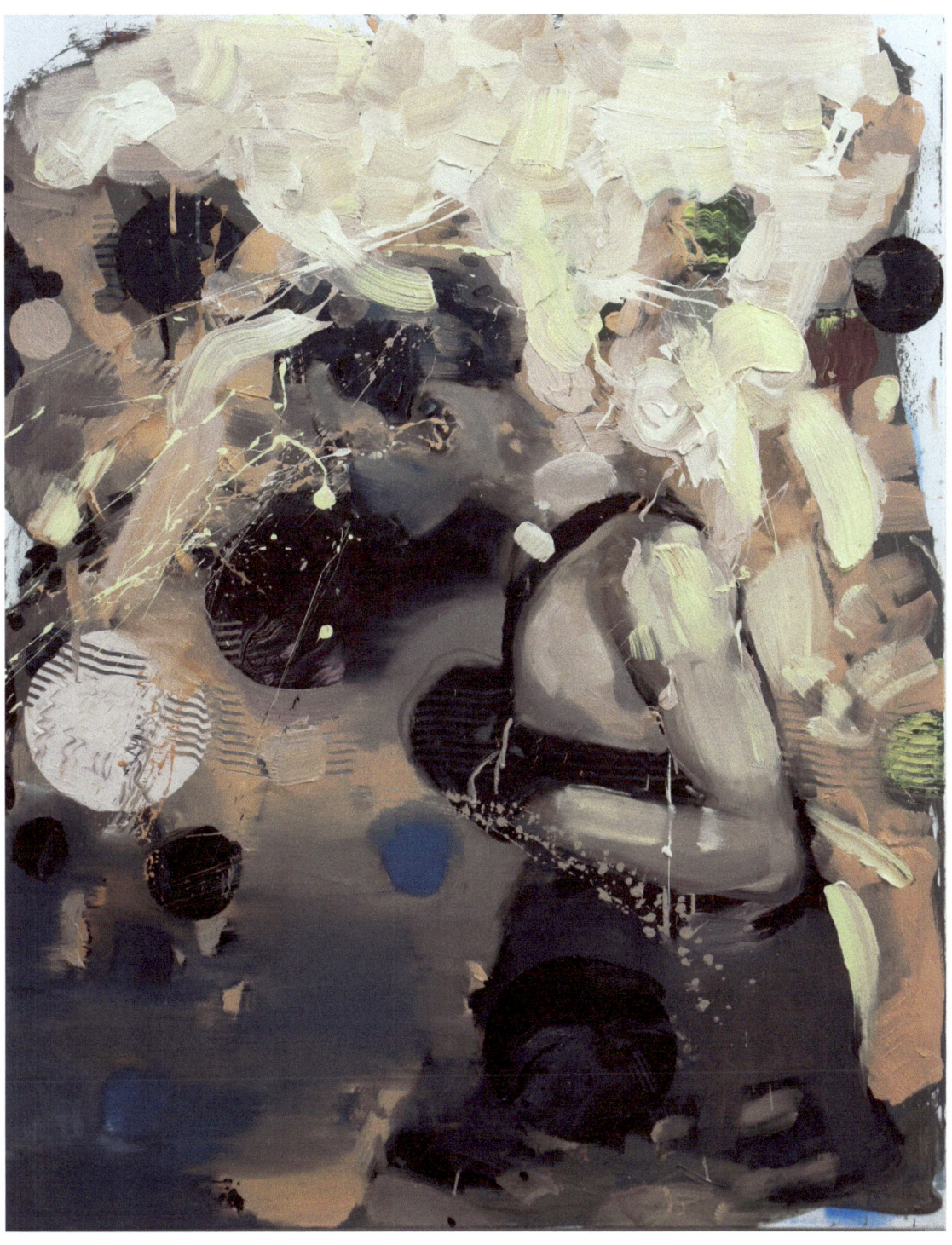

Silent Interior I

oil on panel

38x28cm

2015

Silent Interior III

oil on panel

38x28cm

2015

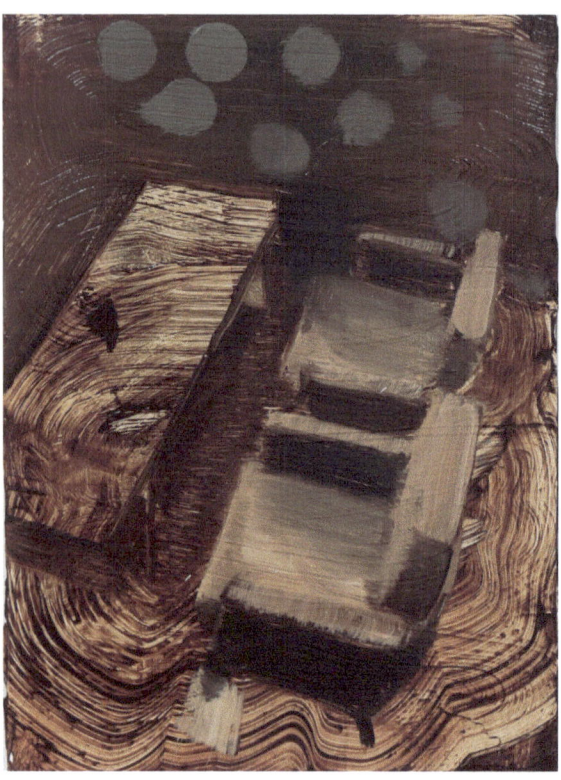 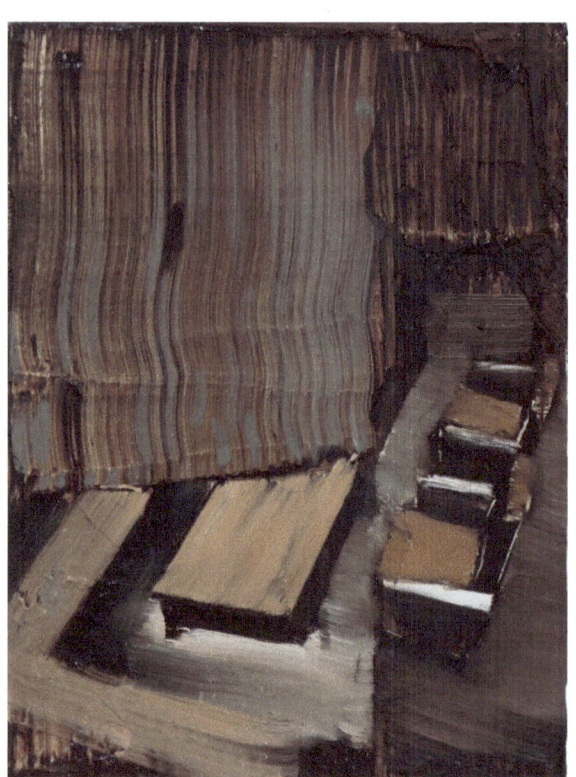

Silent Interior II

oil on panel

38x28cm

2015

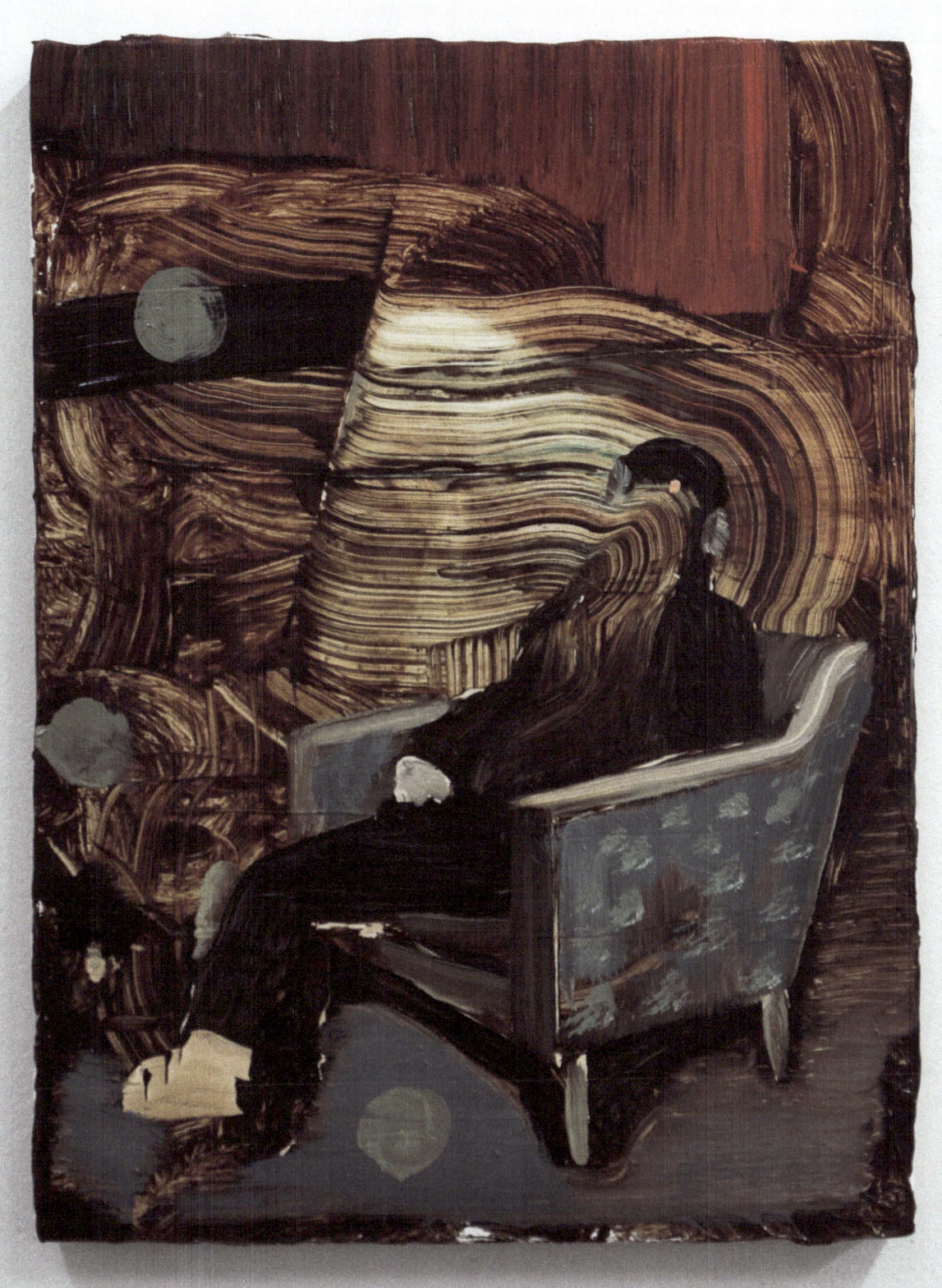

Stream Face I

oil on panel

38x28cm

2015

Stream Face II

oil on panel

38x28cm

2015

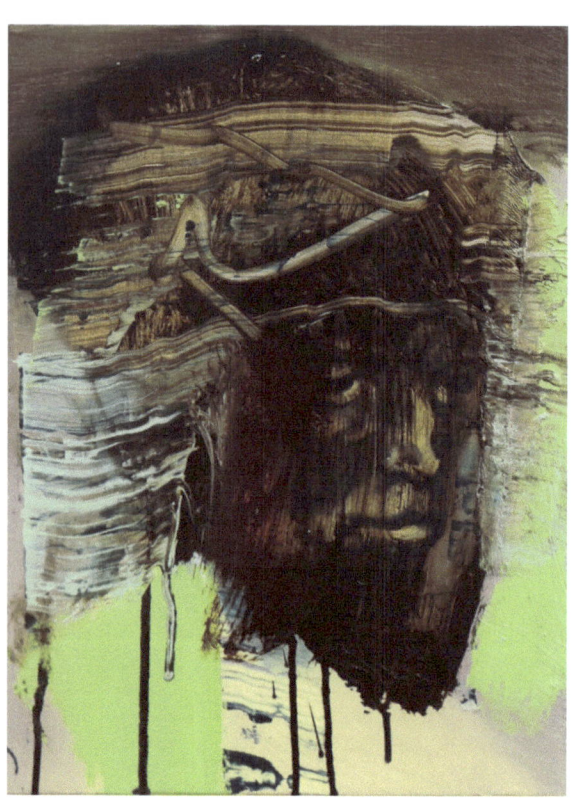 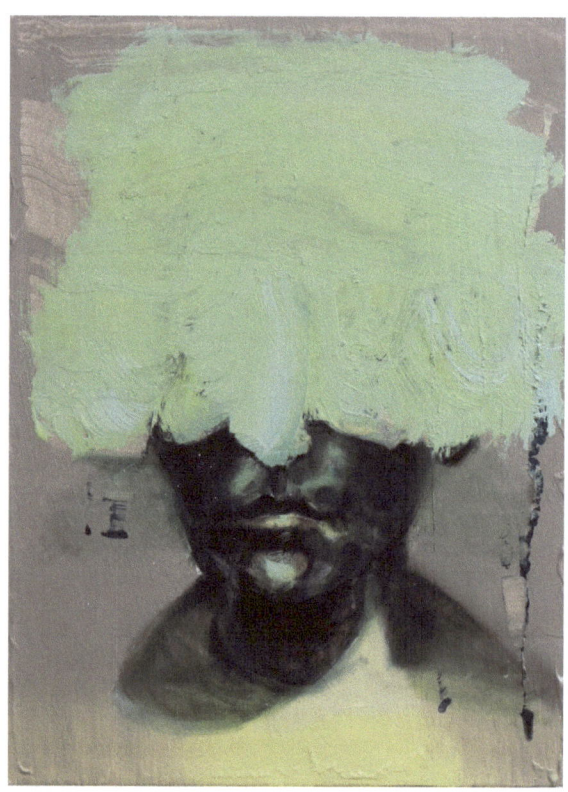

Stream Face I

oil on panel

38x28cm

2015

Stream Face II

oil on panel

38x28cm

2015

Philosophical, psychological or political?

Every time I reconsider any of the individual images, I find myself re-perceiving the collection as a whole. I'm conscious of my own limitations of seeing and how this art not only absorbs that consciousness, but insists on my absorbing it back. I can't help asking if Beda's art is making an intimate or a public statement calling for an internal or judgmental examination. Has he assumed authority over his subject, and/or over the viewer, or is he too, experiencing the anguish, struggling with his own urgent narrative as he "destroys" in order to create?

—*"Encountering Bartosz Beda: It's Personal" by Georgia Tiffany, Expose Magazine, October 2015*

Flat Emotion I

oil on canvas

168x120cm

2015

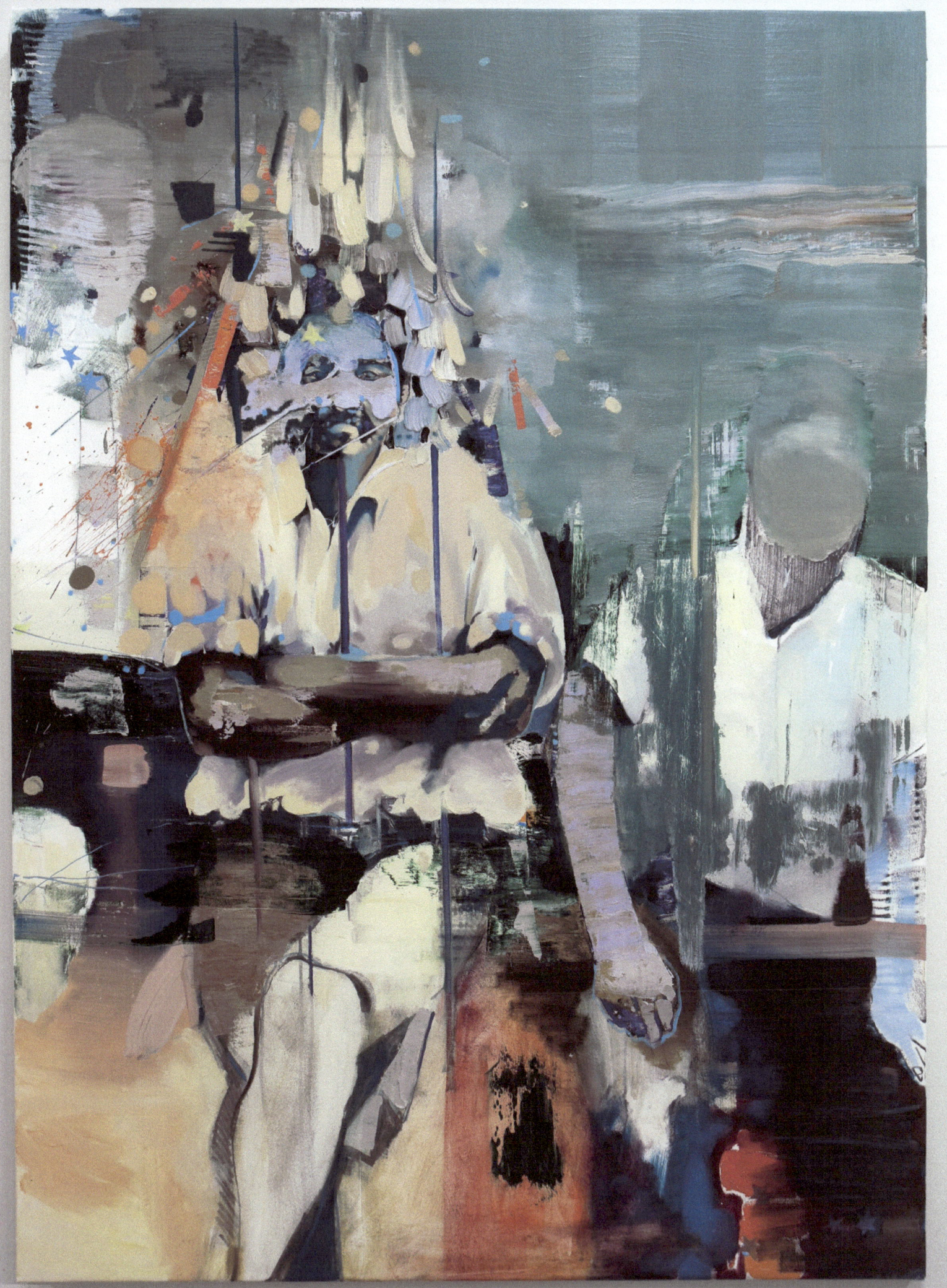

Flat Emotion II

oil on canvas

145x120cm

2015

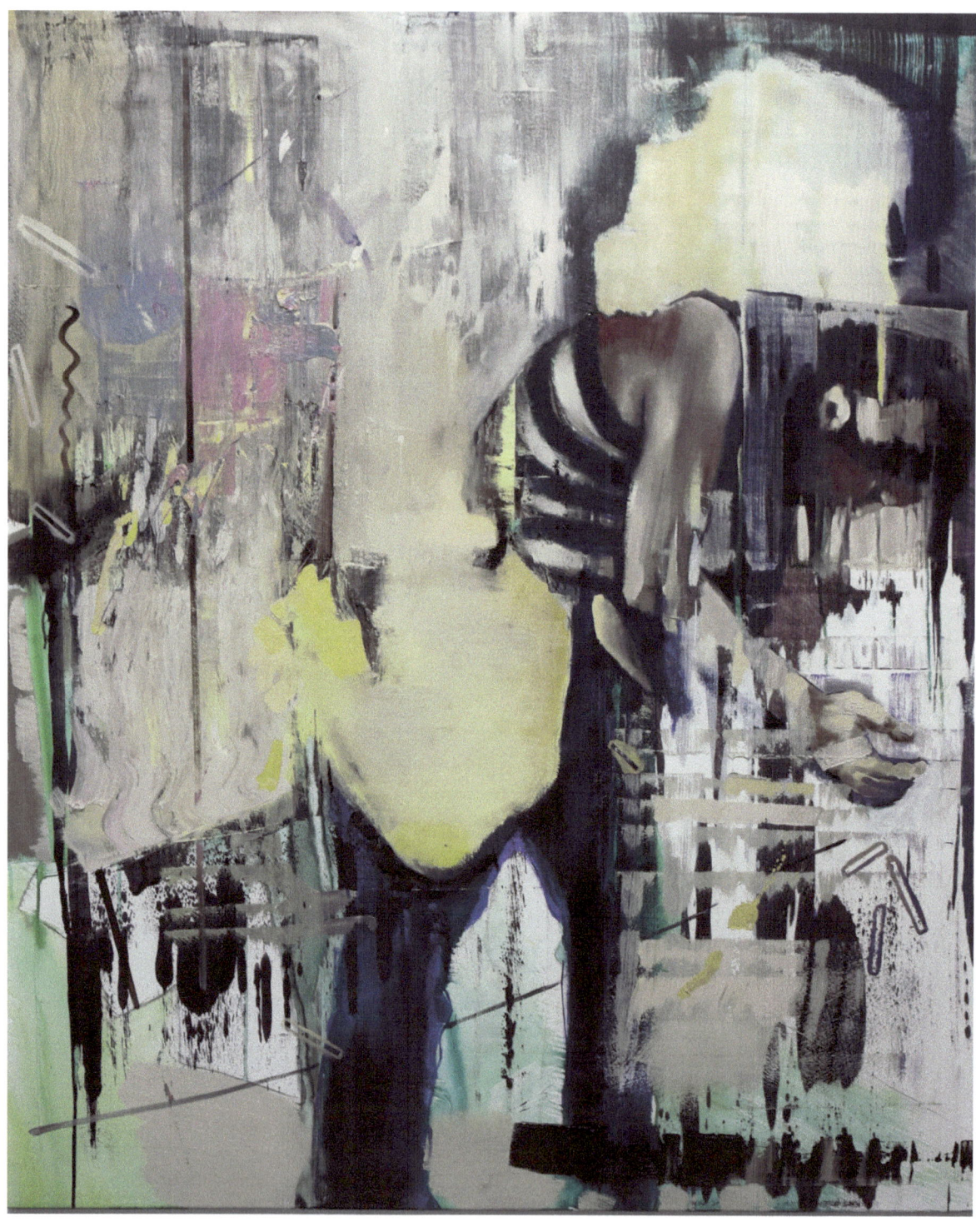

Labor I and II

oil on panel

40x40cm

2015

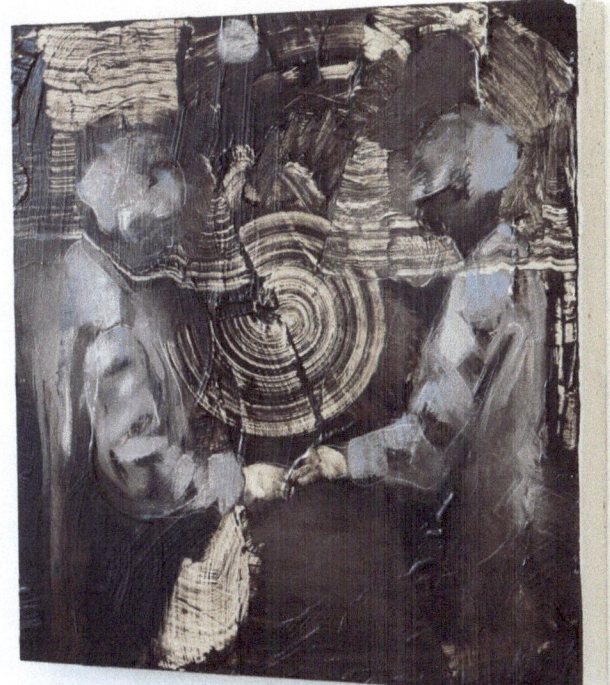
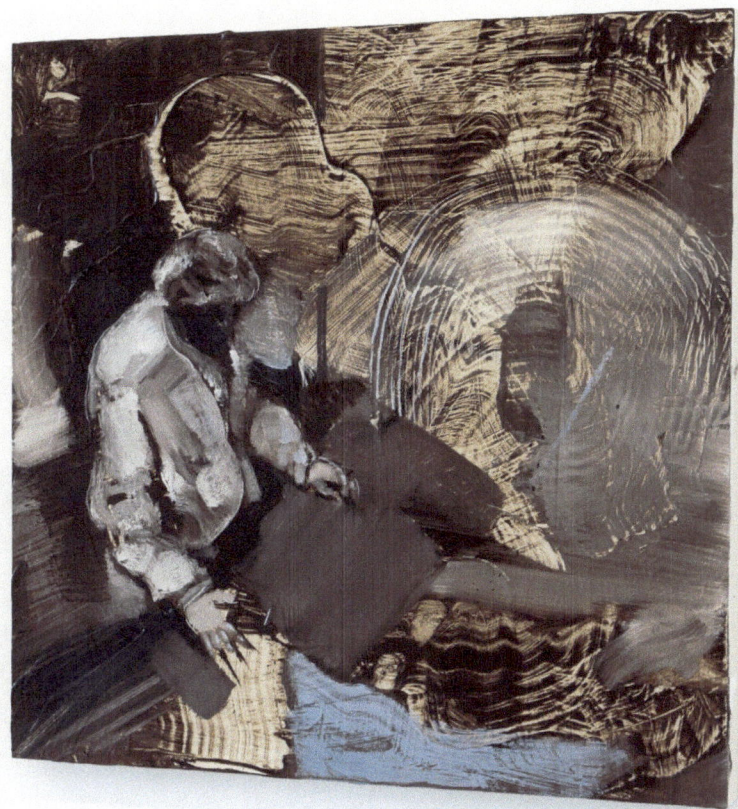

Idol II

oil on canvas

32x23cm

2015

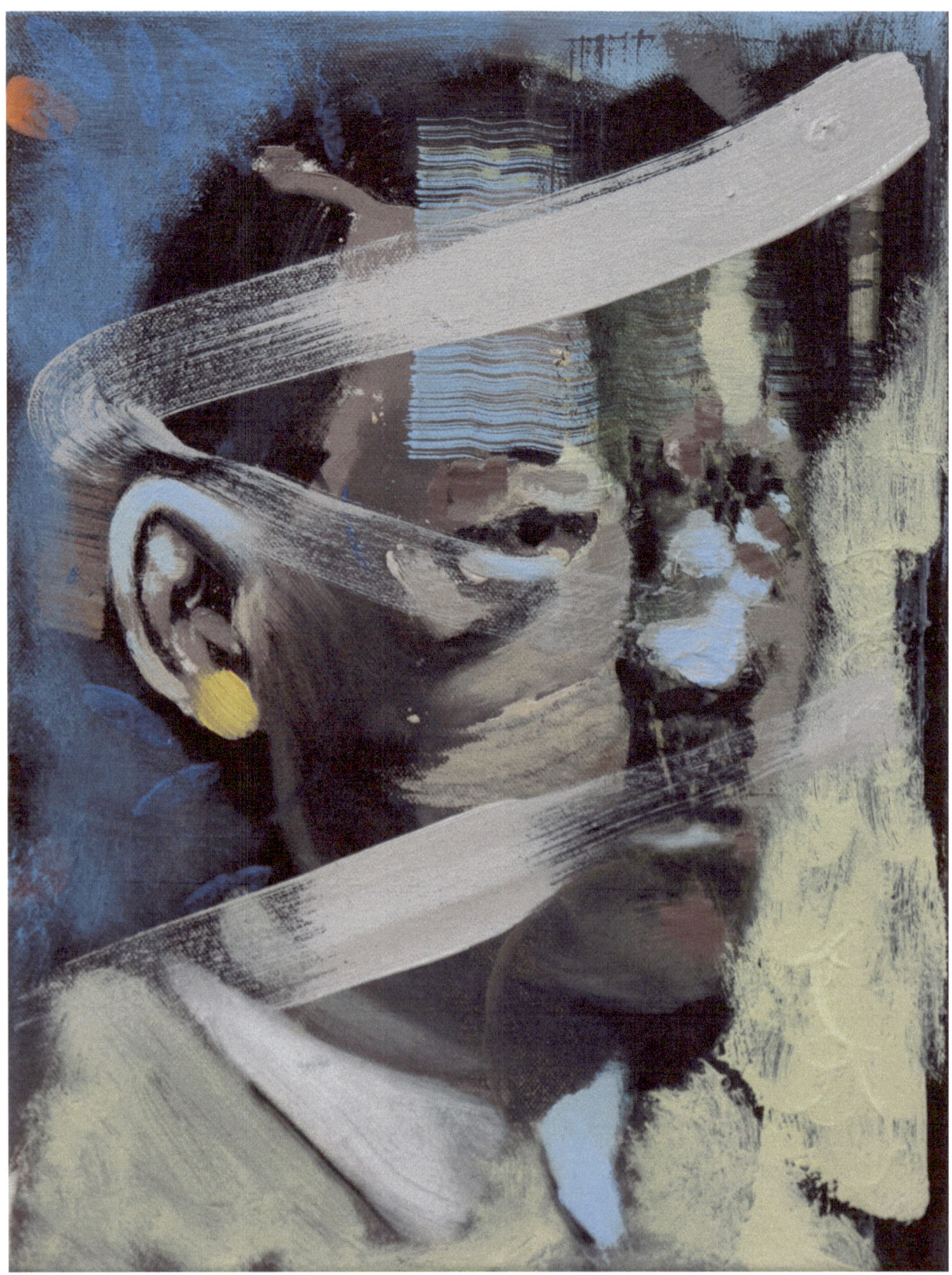

Flat Emotion III

oil on canvas

127x107cm

2015

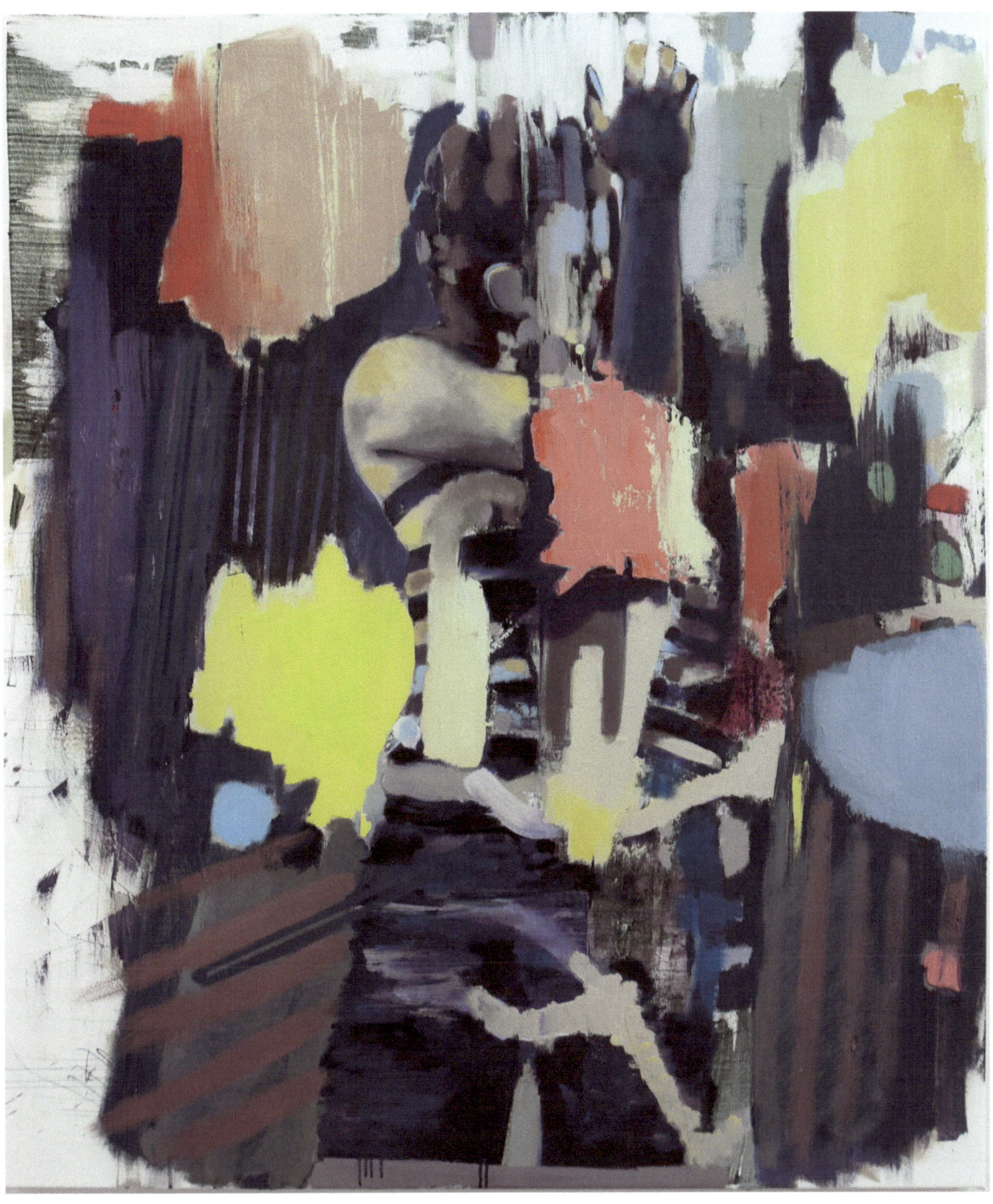

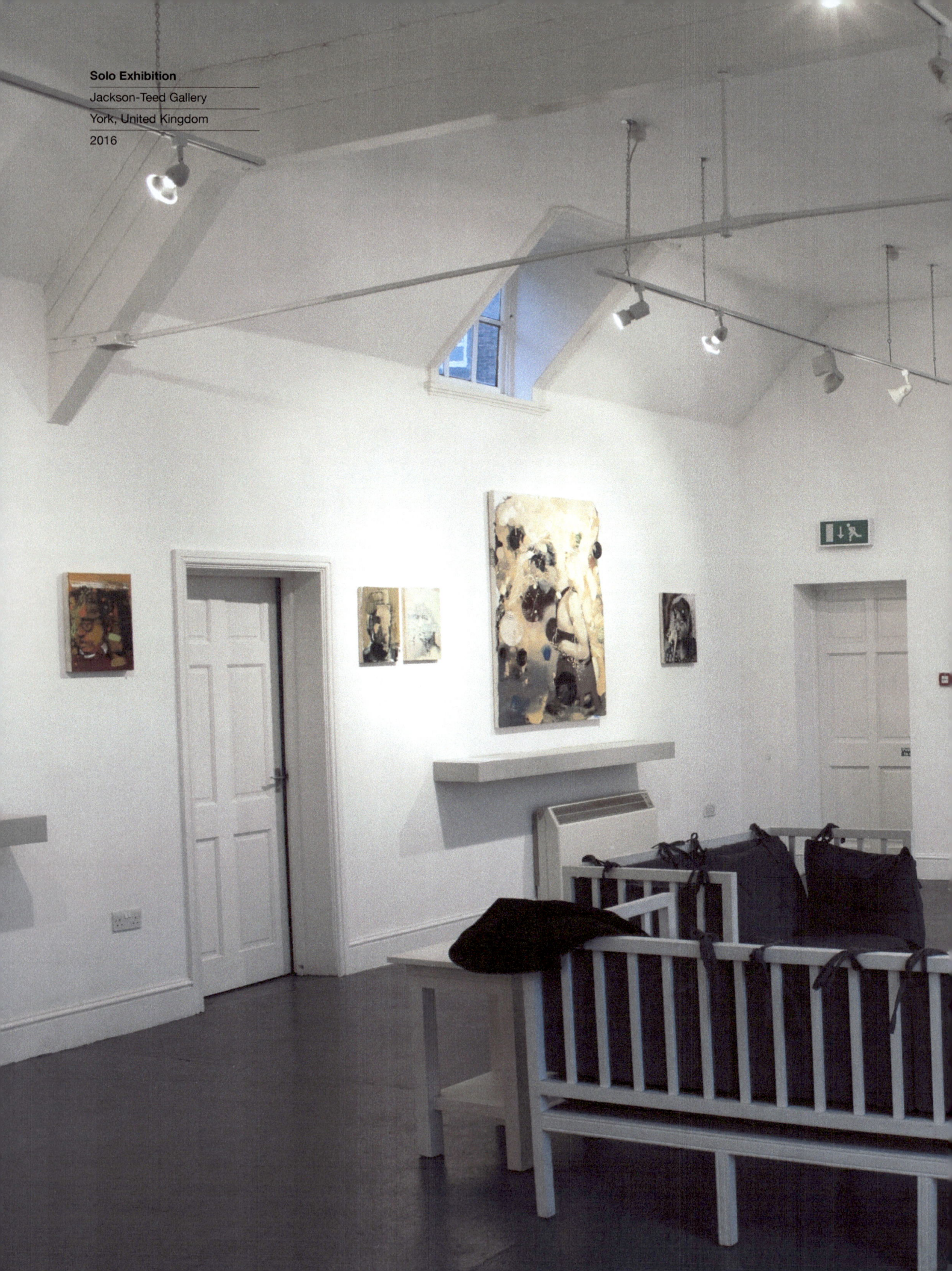

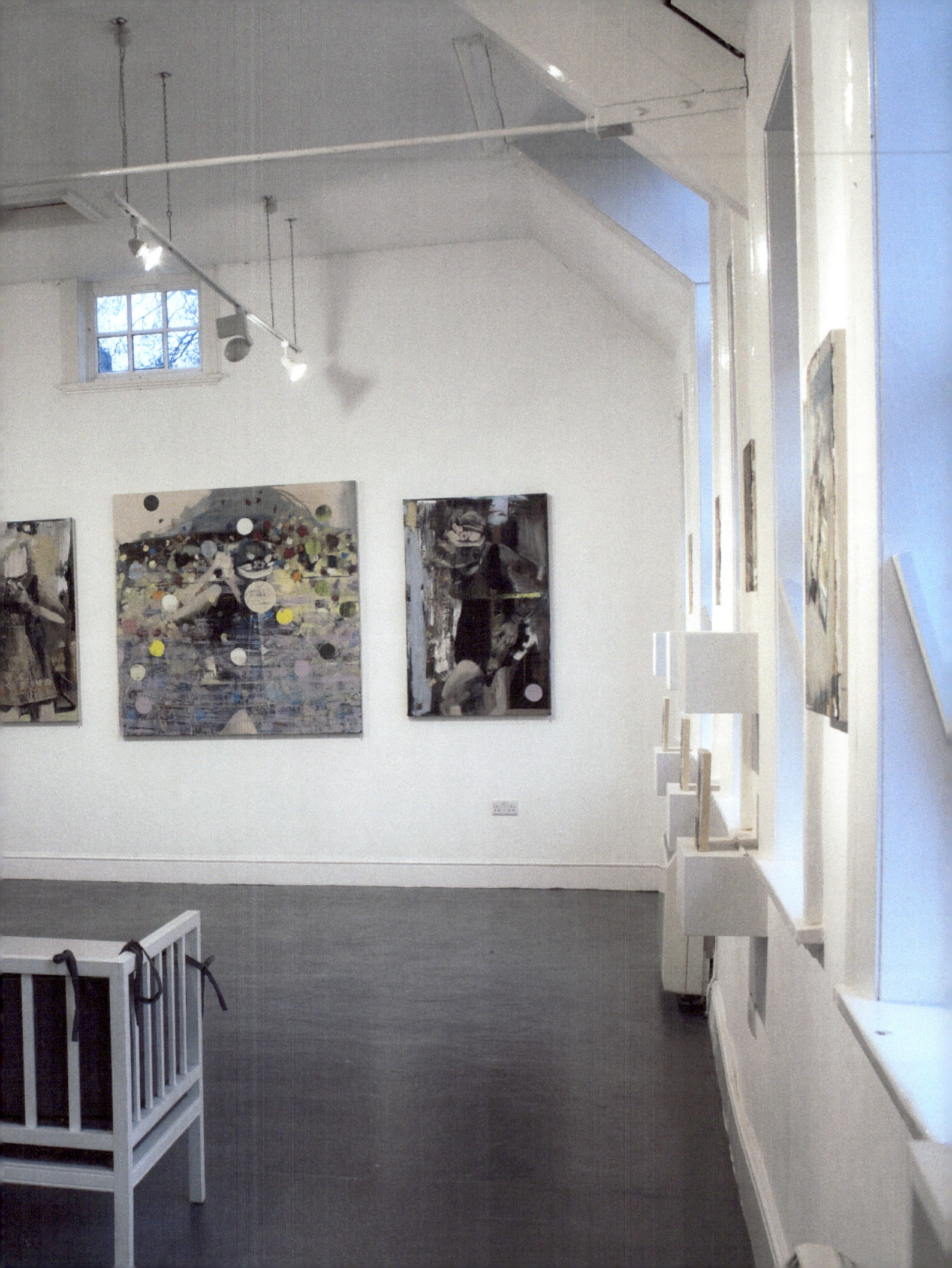

Emerging Series

Emerging I

oil on canvas

48x36cm

2016

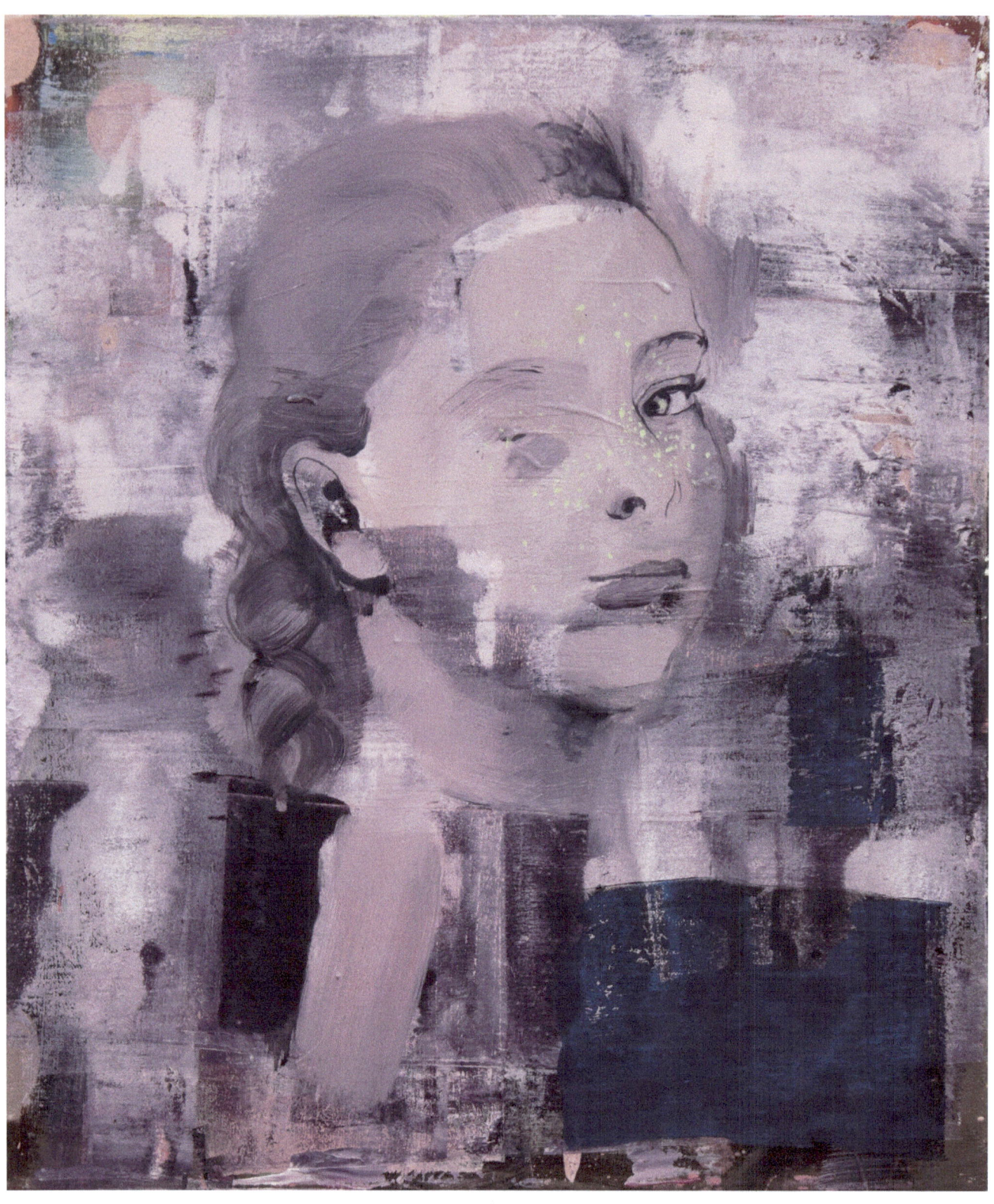

Emerging II

oil on canvas

48x36cm

2016

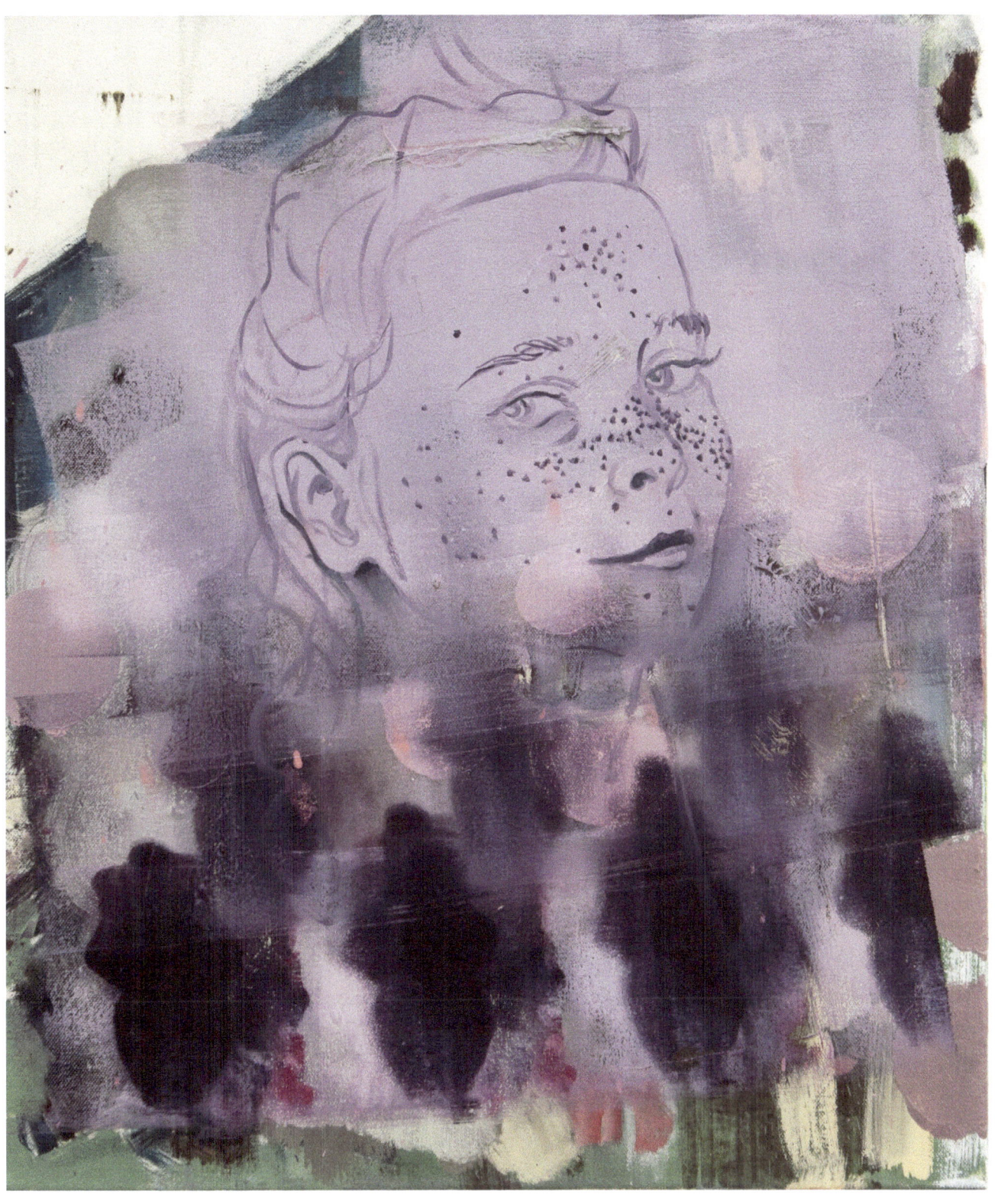

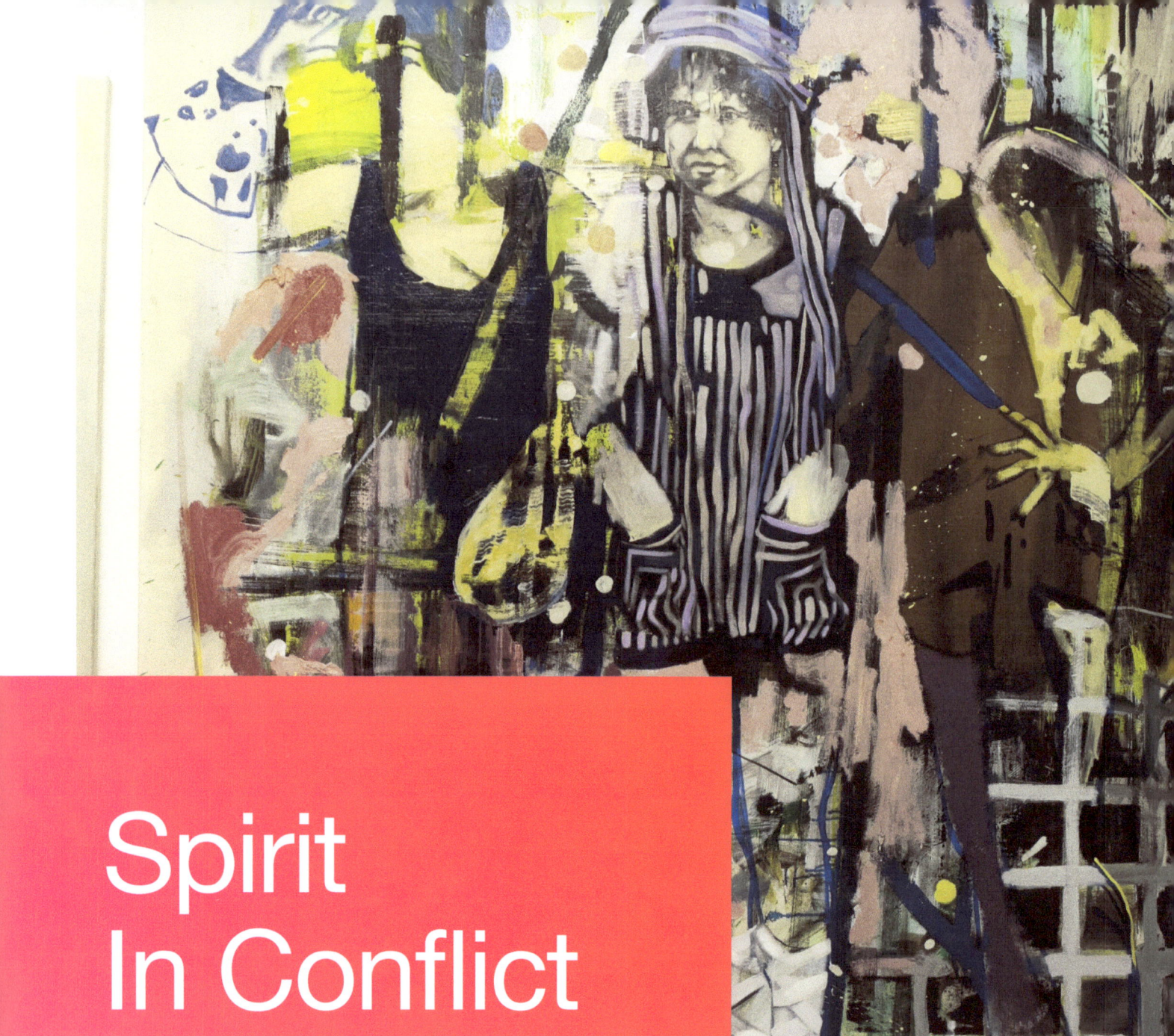

Spirit
In Conflict

by Georgia Tiffany

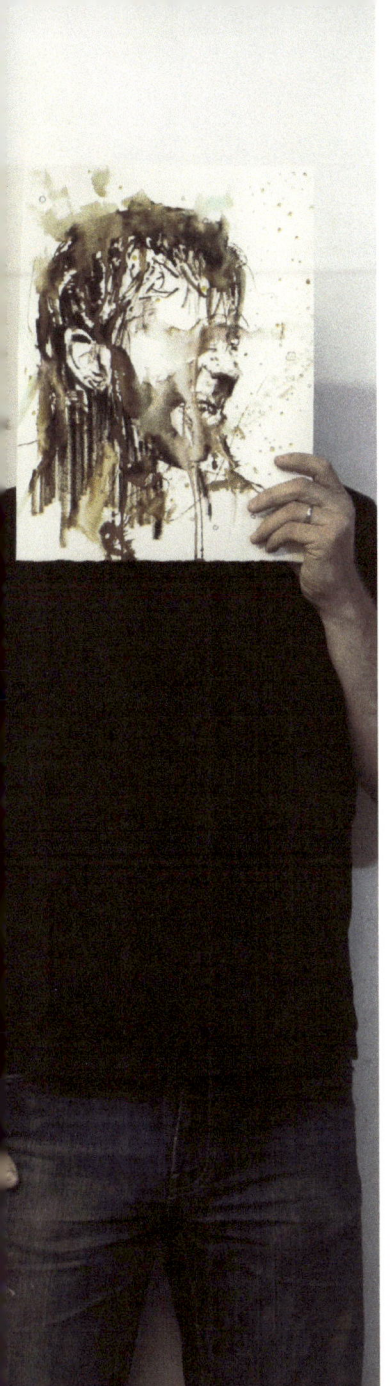

We wear the mask that grins and lies,
It hides our cheeks and shades our eyes,—
This debt we pay to human guile;
With torn and bleeding hearts we smile,
And mouth with myriad subtleties.

— Paul Laurence Dunbar

The role of artists, says Anton Chekhov, is to ask questions, not to answer them. By implication then, is it our role as viewers to seek the answers? Or, ultimately, does the search itself become the meaning.

Bartosz Beda vigorously assumes Chekhov's role of the artist. To stand before one of Beda's painting is to be challenged by an intense, even intimidating energy. The multi-layers of paint, and stroke, and image, insist that we engage. His art compels a search for meaning that not only transcends the representational success and materiality of his painting, but the space around it as well. It is an encounter of consciousness that can haunt us long after we turn from the work. As a result of his questions, we do not stop asking our own. Beda expects a lot from us. His art explores the inward significance of the quotidian and the spiritual, the significance of conflict and the extent we embrace or deny it. Beda's art disturbs the peace.

And he dares to take us into the political. "What do you think an artist is?" asks Picasso, and answers, "...he is a political being, constantly aware of the heart breaking, passionate, or delightful things that happen in the world, shaping himself completely in their image. Painting is not done to decorate apartments. It is an instrument of war."

Beda admits his work is often inspired by such moments, but his paintings are not "about" those moments. They simply serve, he maintains, as places to start on an artistic journey.

According to Beda, the very act of producing the work distorts the initial motivation to create it, distorts the point from which the artistic journey begins by the way it materializes on the canvas. Even the very surface on which the painting appears distorts the artist's incipient impulse by the completion of the work. However, or as a result, because an artist is distracted by the process of that response, the distraction becomes an essential part of the art.

continued on p. 75

Vacation

oil on canvas

168x120cm

2016

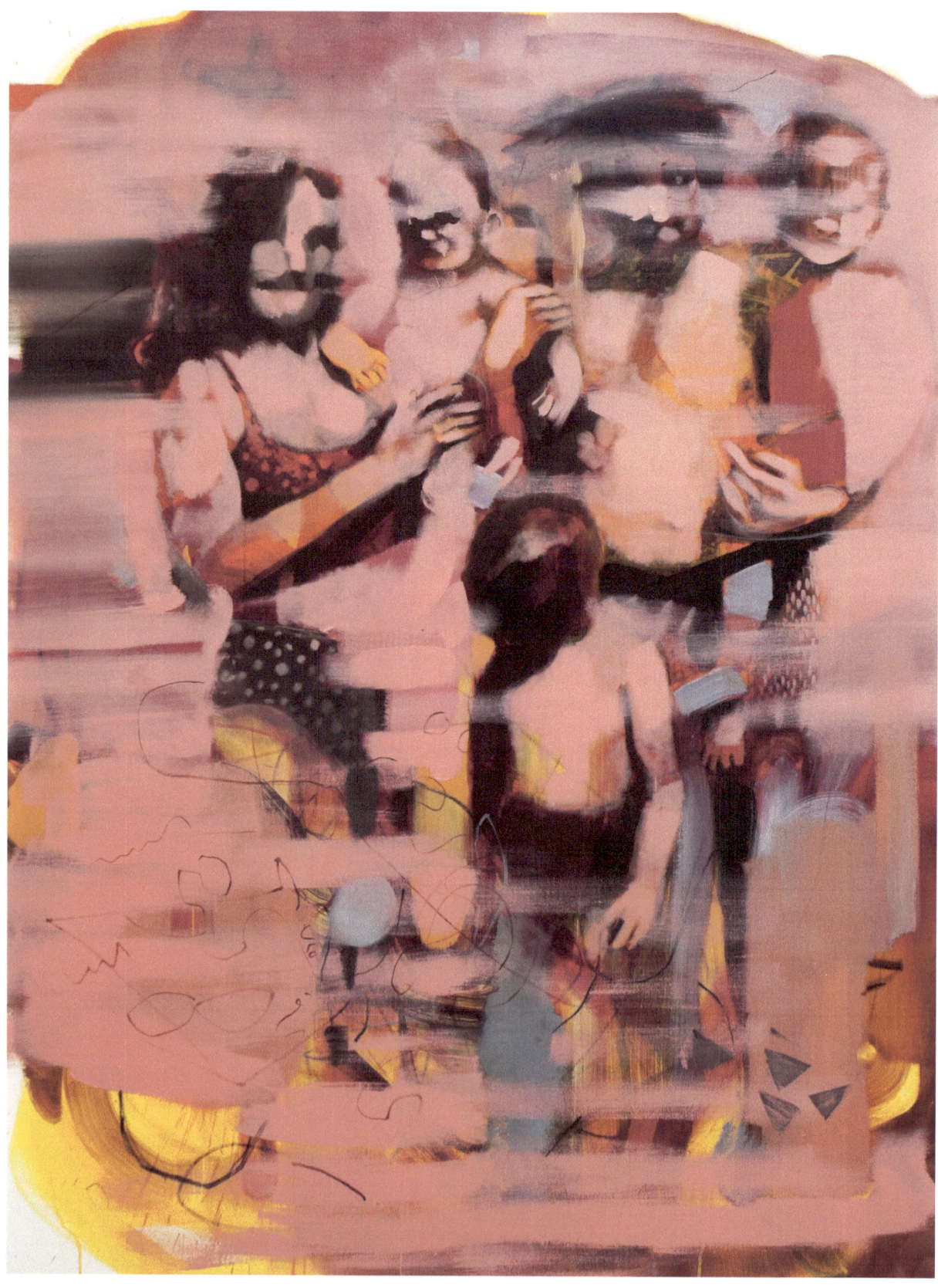

Europa

oil on canvas

178x127cm

2016

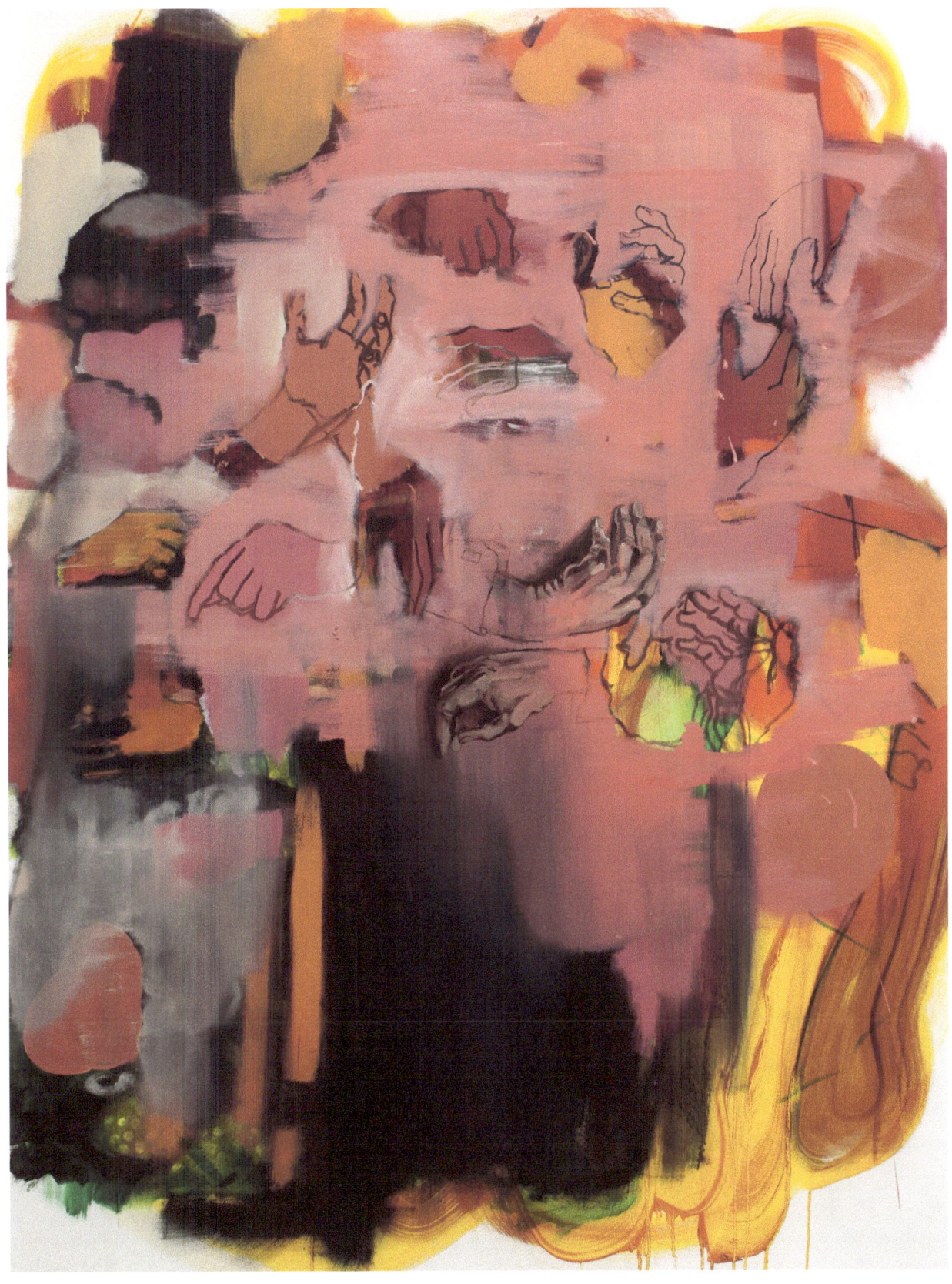

Man of Hope

oil on canvas

178x127cm

2016

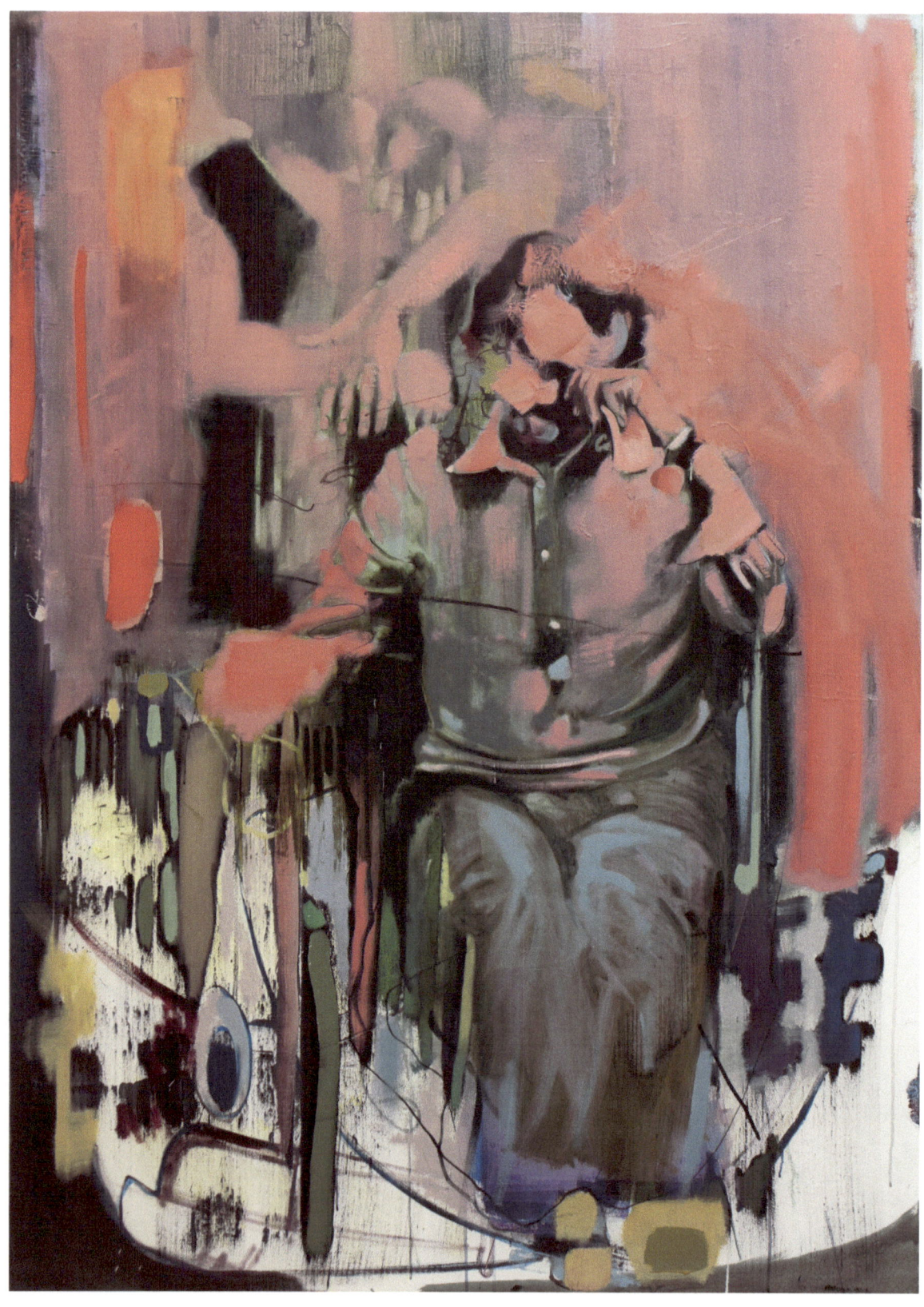

Man of Hope

oil on canvas

46x38cm

2016

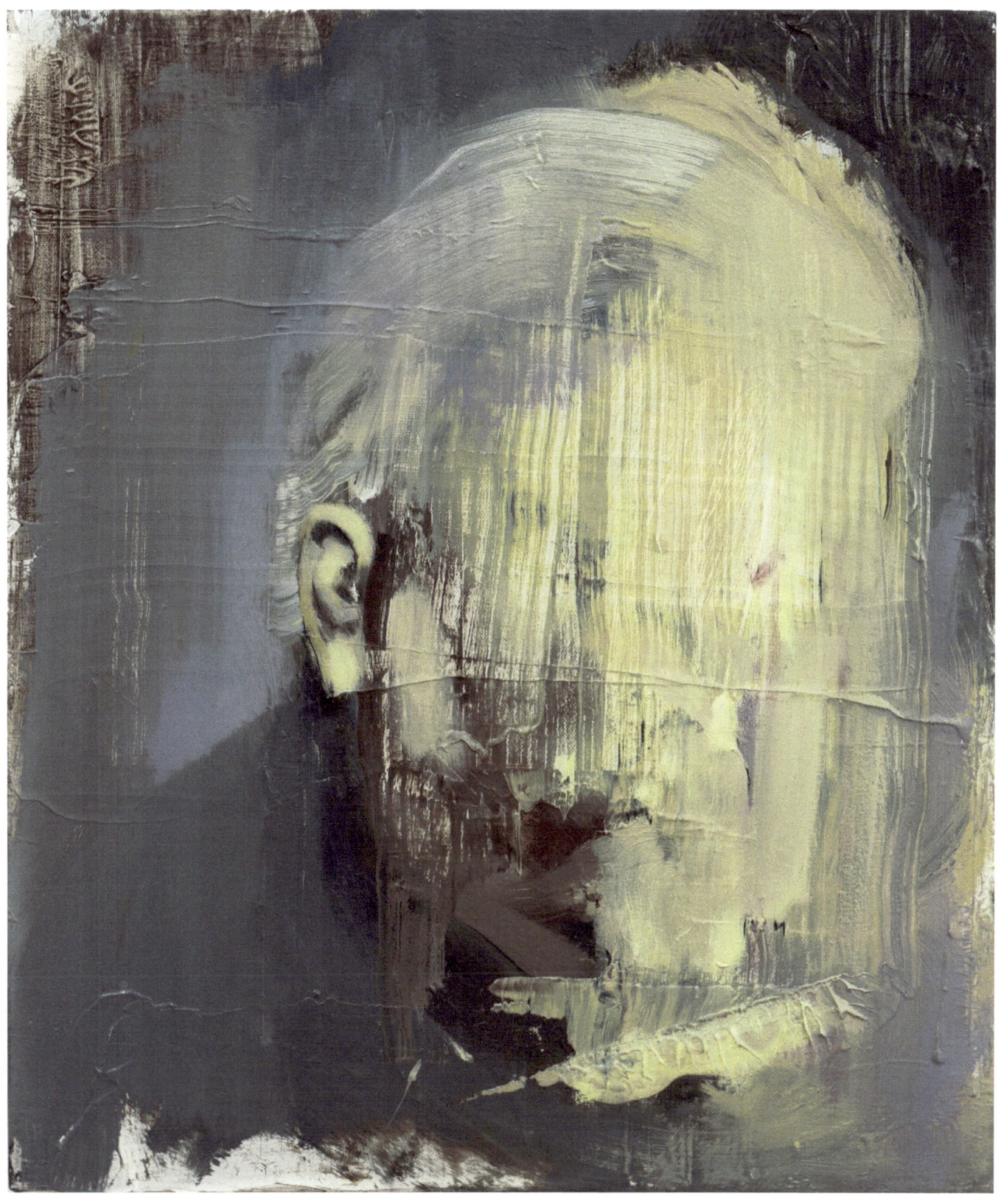

Untitled III

oil on canvas

36x28cm

2016

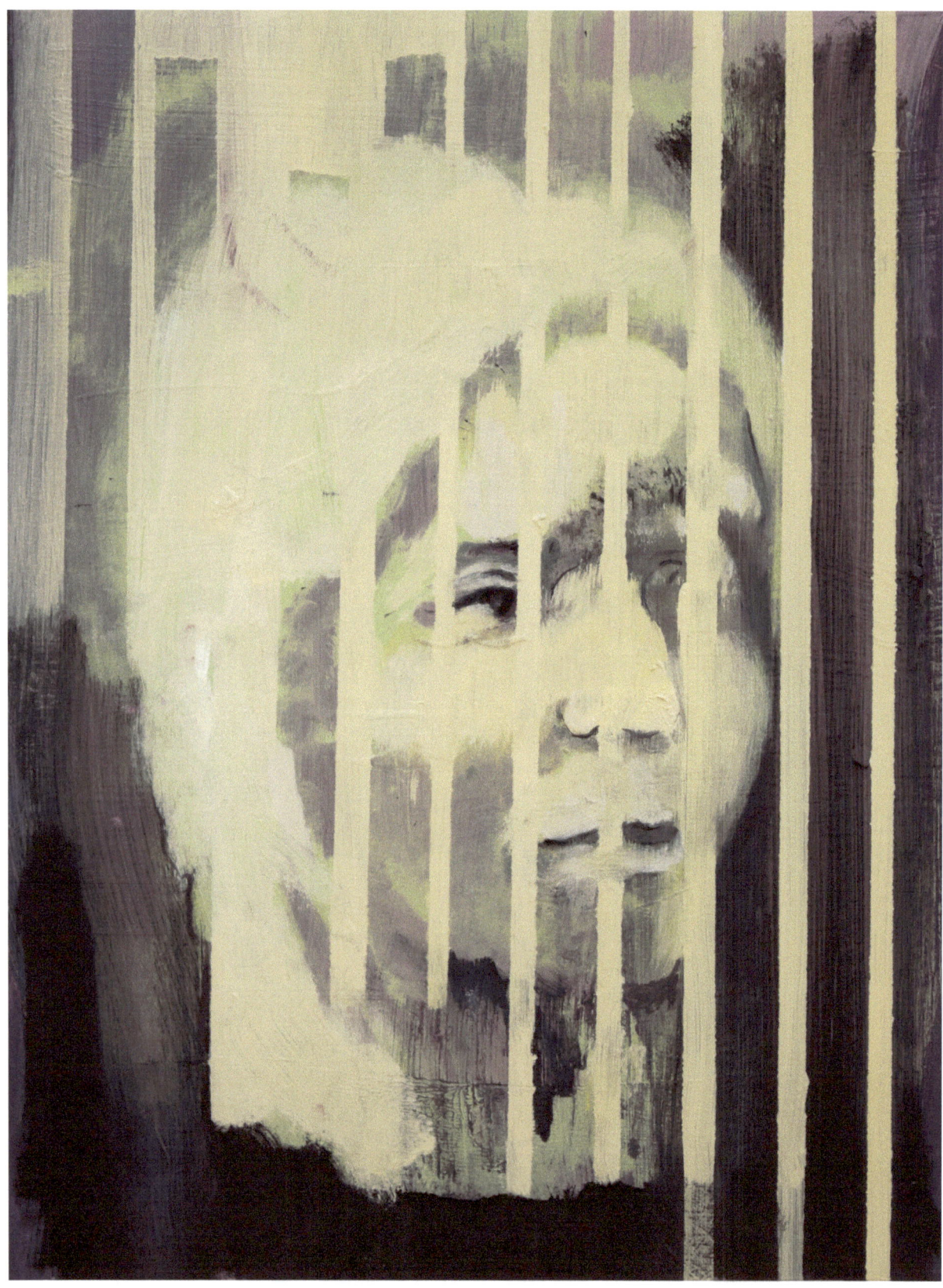

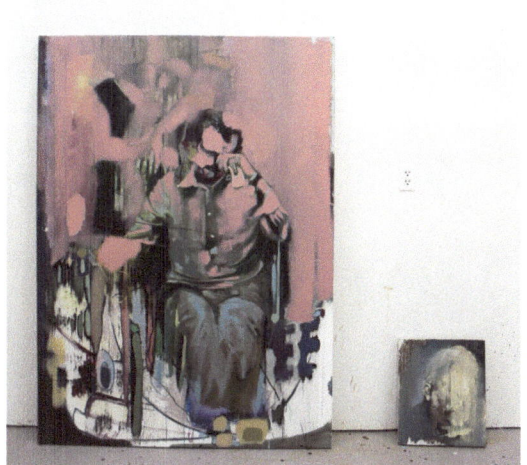

Three of Bartosz Beda's politically motivated paintings from 2016, displayed together at a show in Spokane, Washington, evolved out of the recent challenges of democracy in Europe and around the world. They have a monumental presence and bear ironic titles which underscore their impact. *Europa* (see p. 71) isolates and alienates an assortment of unmatched hands—reaching, pointing, fisted, distorted, arthritic—that do not touch each other with only one exception, and that exception perhaps an allusion to Michelangelo's *Creation of Adam*. Another painting inspired by the former President of Poland, Lech Walesa, shows a seated figure leaning his head on his hand, the hand poised as if to wipe away a tear. His body, a language of defeat. Menacing hands detected in the otherwise negative space droop down from some unseen figure (or ghost?) above him. Title: *Man of Hope* (see p.72) The third painting, *Vacation* (see p.70), depicts Lech Walesa's family of five posed for a photo at the beach. Their eyes sink darkly into the paint or are obscured. Their mouths, when visible, are grim. These three paintings conspire for unity through their exact same size (168 x 120 cm), their predominantly bright variations of pink, and their depiction of hands.

One cannot help wondering what is hidden, as if each painting as it appears is a kind of mask behind which other paintings had surrendered to the final images and colors. What is hidden is almost palpable.

Another series of political paintings consists of naked human figures in blue masks. Beda explains that the mask evolved as a kind of metaphor of the conflict in Ukraine, but he stresses that the paintings are not "about" that conflict. He sees the masks as an attempt at anonymity in human interaction with that conflict, and the absurdity of the intention to do so. We ultimately find ourselves not so much a part of the conflict, as a part of the futility of it all. Masks and illusion, absurdity and futility. Who we are in the world is not who we would be.

In this 2014 series, Beda produced six oils of life-size figures with blue masks. From the primal nudity of the squatting humans to their grip on the oddly realistic crosses, from the hands which may or may not be bound together, to the striped chair and manmade star, to the eventual encapsulation of the self-embracing figures in the cells of the *Extraordinius* (see p.30-31) paintings, the journey he takes us on insists we look and look again. As with all of Bartosz Beda's work, these paintings insist we see.

If, as George Bernard Shaw says in *Back to Methuselah*, "You use a glass mirror to see your face; you use works of art to see your soul," then what questions does this series ask us about our souls? "I wear the blue mask, too," Beda explains. "I cannot escape the world I see around me, even as I paint."

From bold raw lines to delicate trails of paint to sensual full-body curves; from pen and ink to oils to squeegies to pyramidical three-dimensional interactive paintings, Bartosz relentlessly experiments. From chairs to trucks, sitting rooms to city-scapes; from open-eyed portraits, to missing heads, to a canvas of hands; from mythical to political to self-portrait and all the myriad subtleties. Who we are in the world is not who we would be. We wear the mask.

Often satirical, always compelling, and yet somehow compassionate revelation that can make you weep, Bartosz Beda's art is the human spirit in conflict.

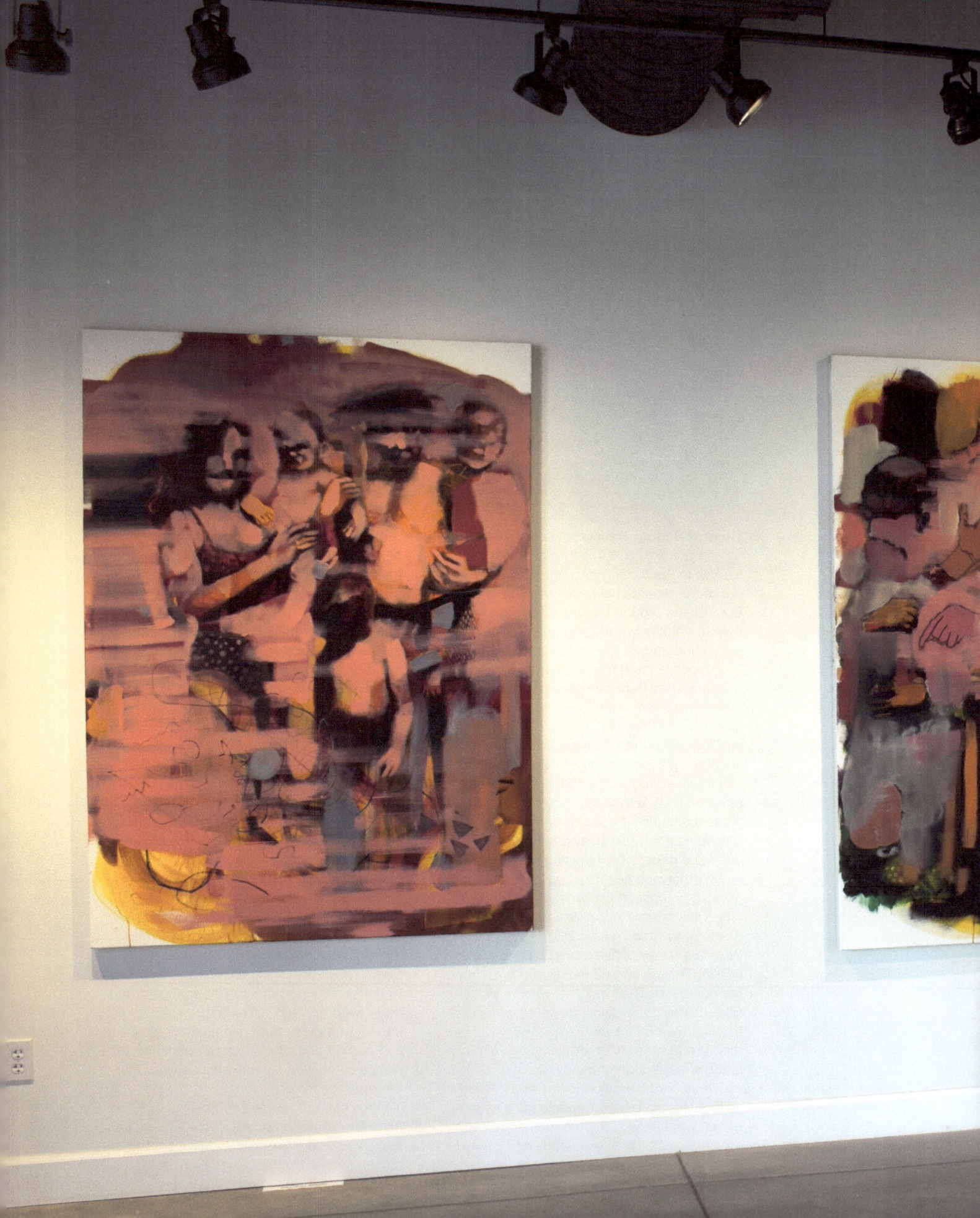

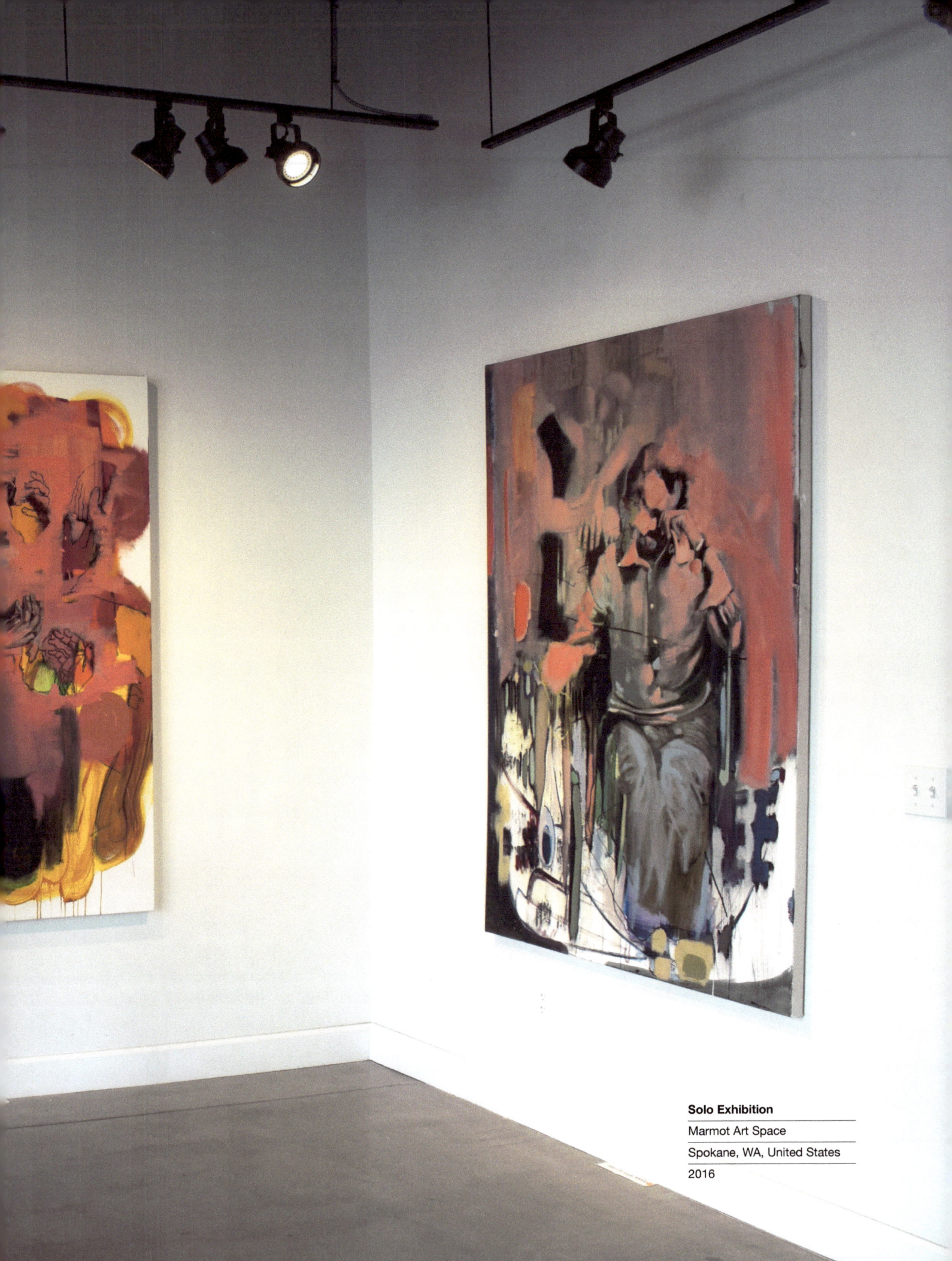

Solo Exhibition

Marmot Art Space

Spokane, WA, United States

2016

Francis Bacon Series

Francis Bacon Fight for Color

oil on canvas

151x155cm

2016

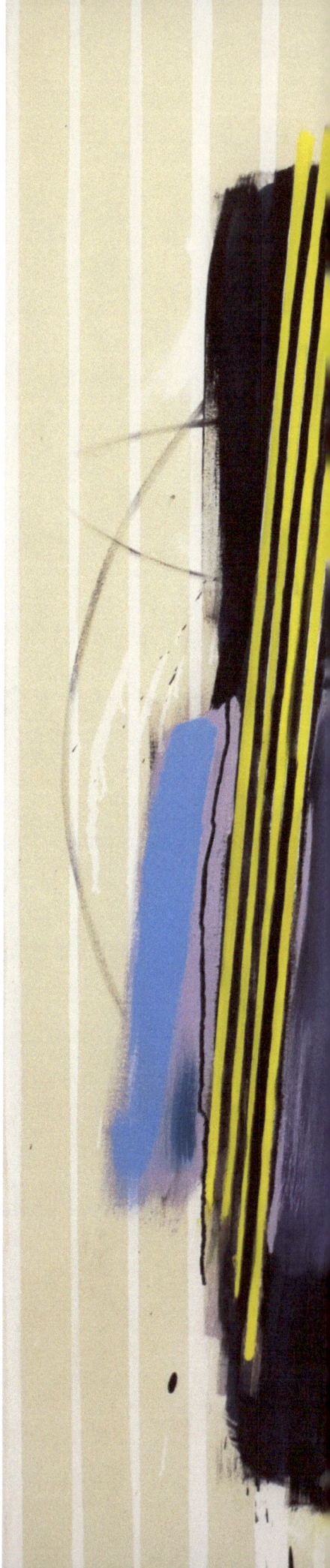

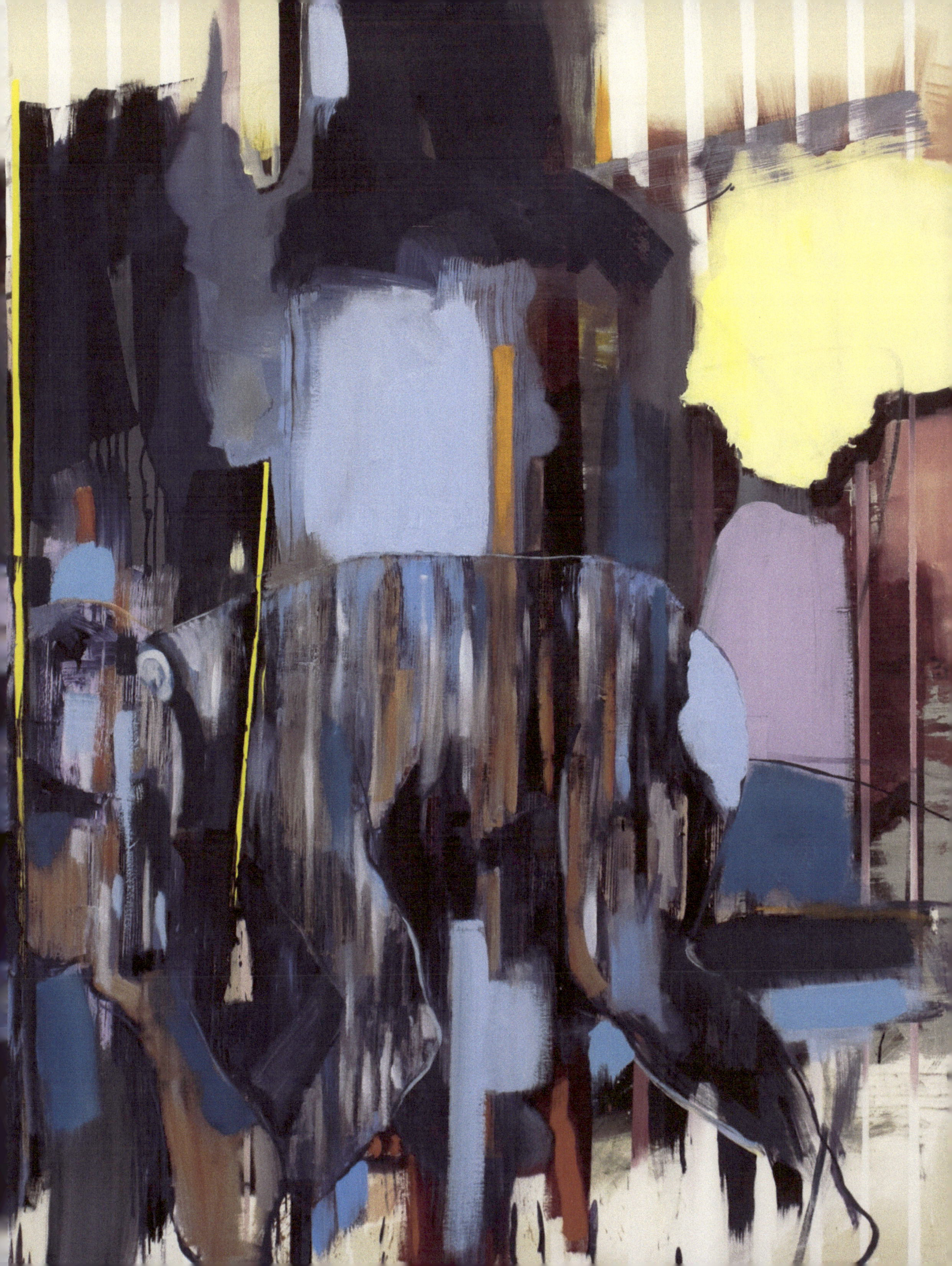

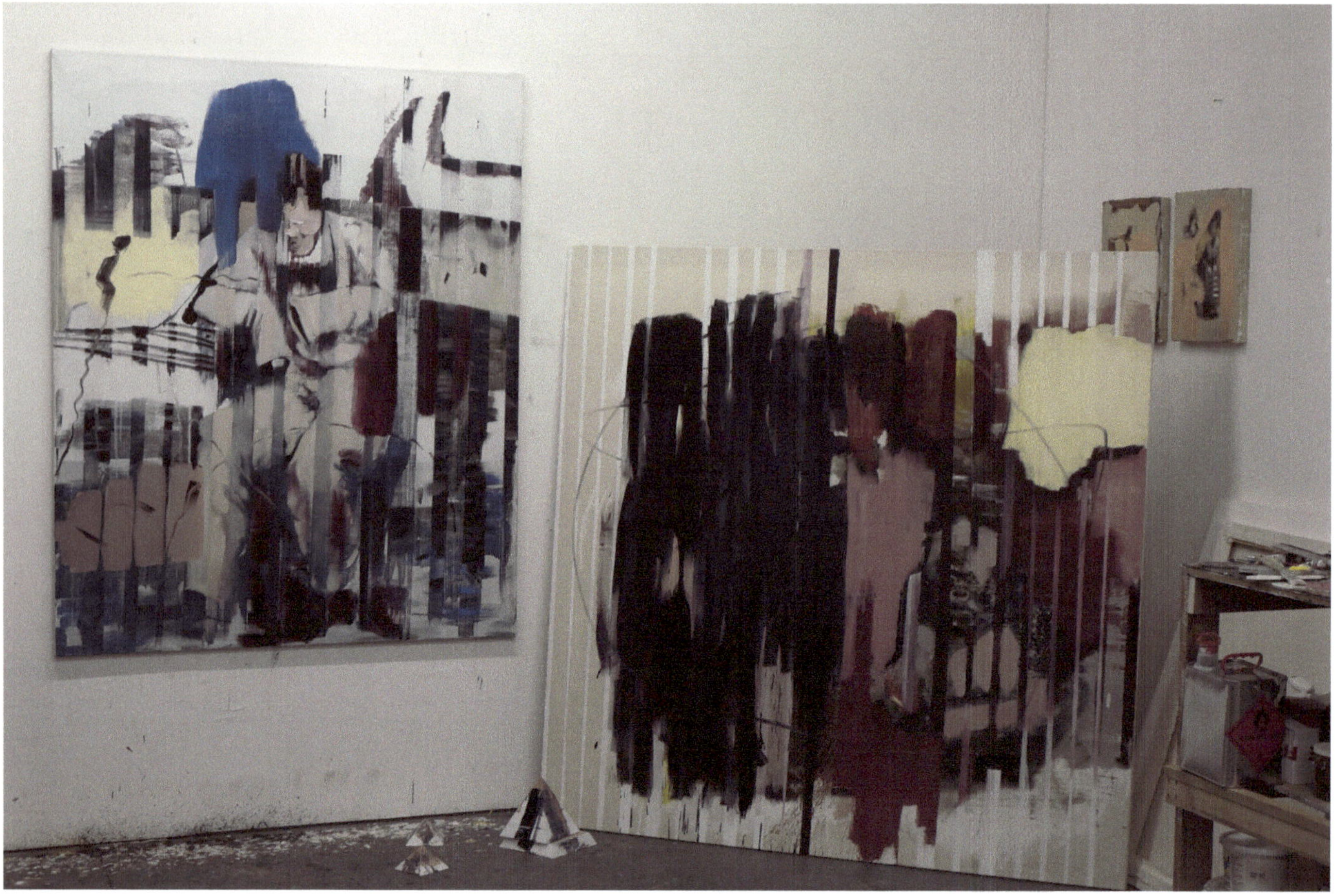

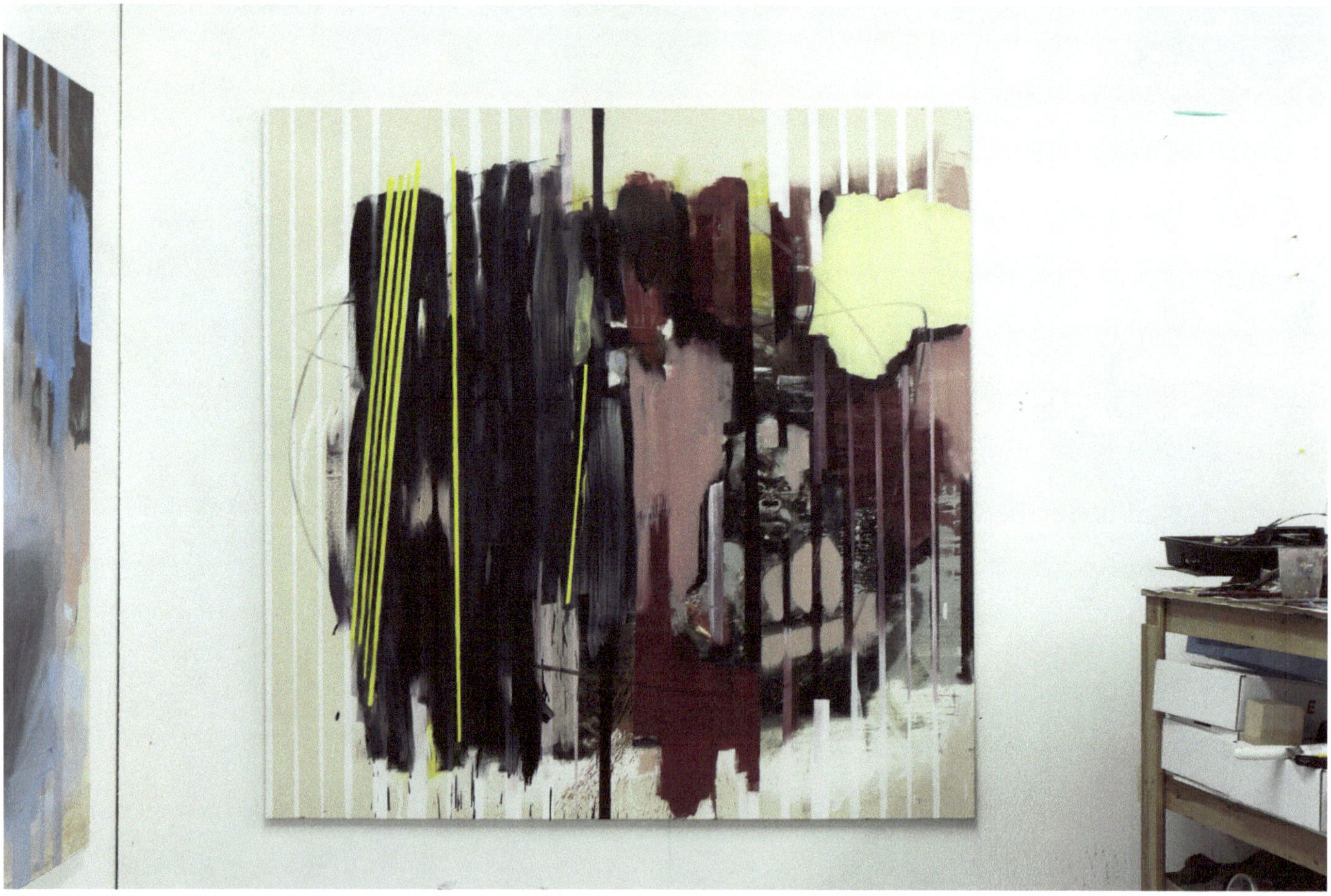

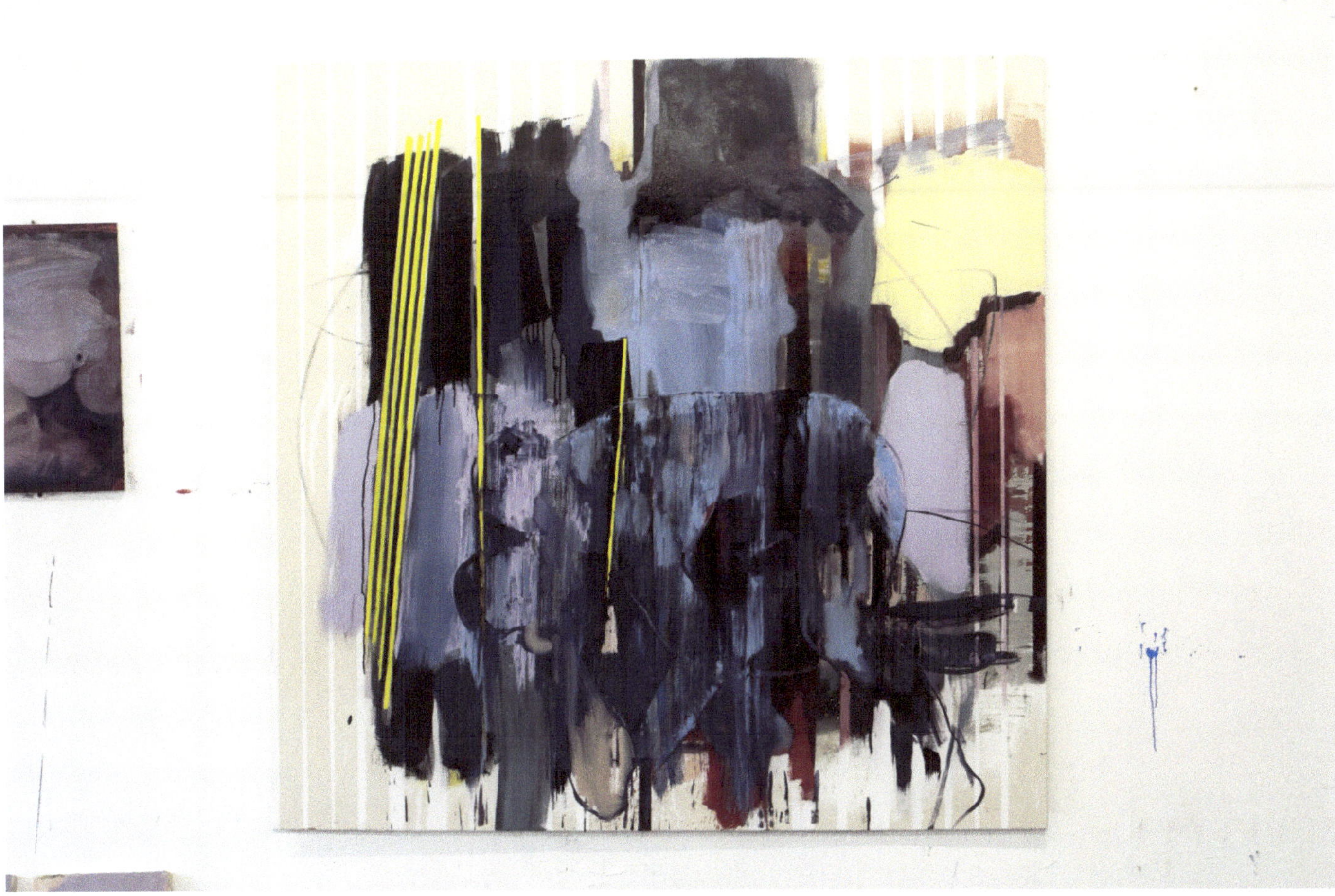

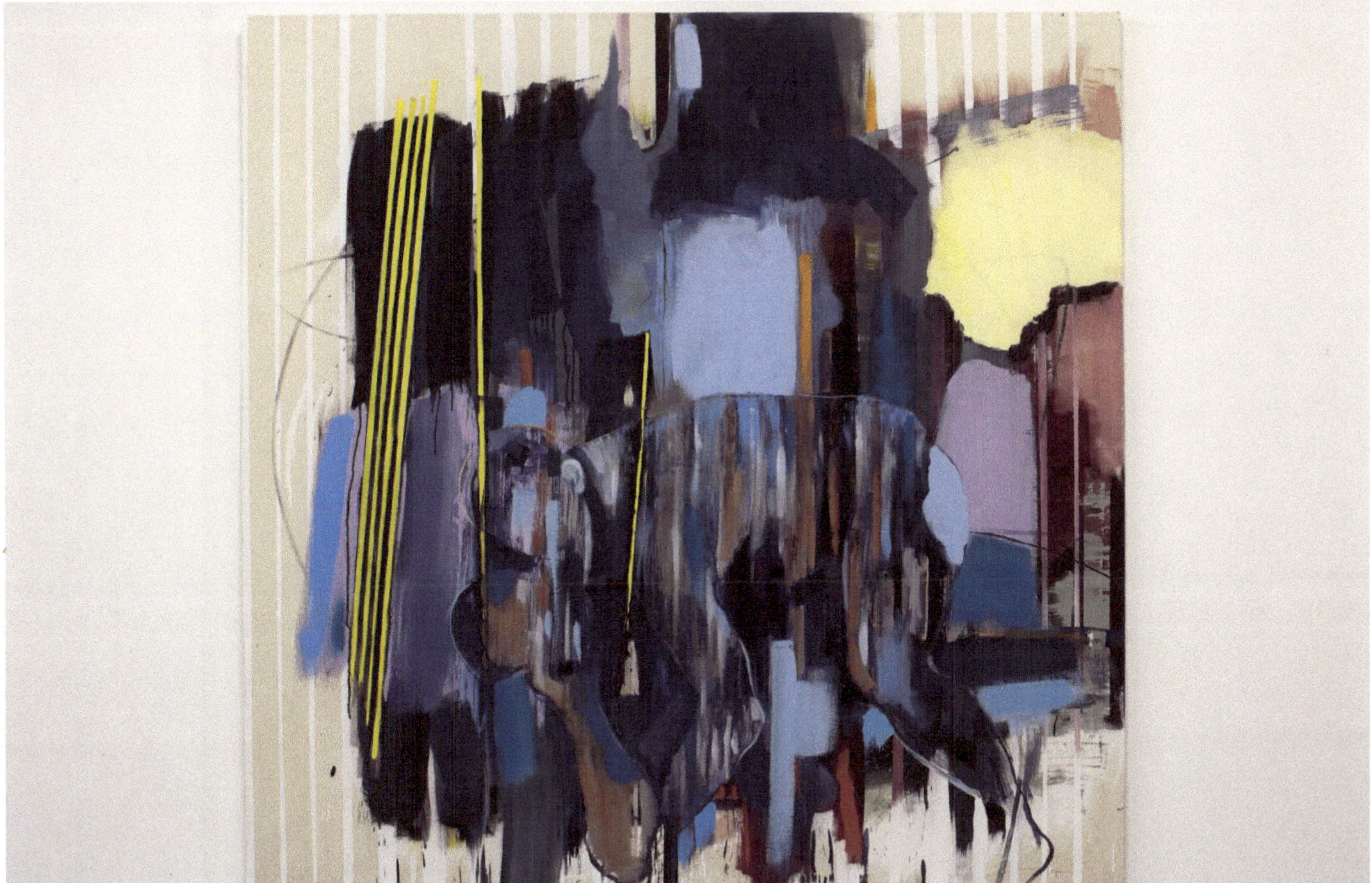

Man in Blue

oil on canvas

150x120cm

2016

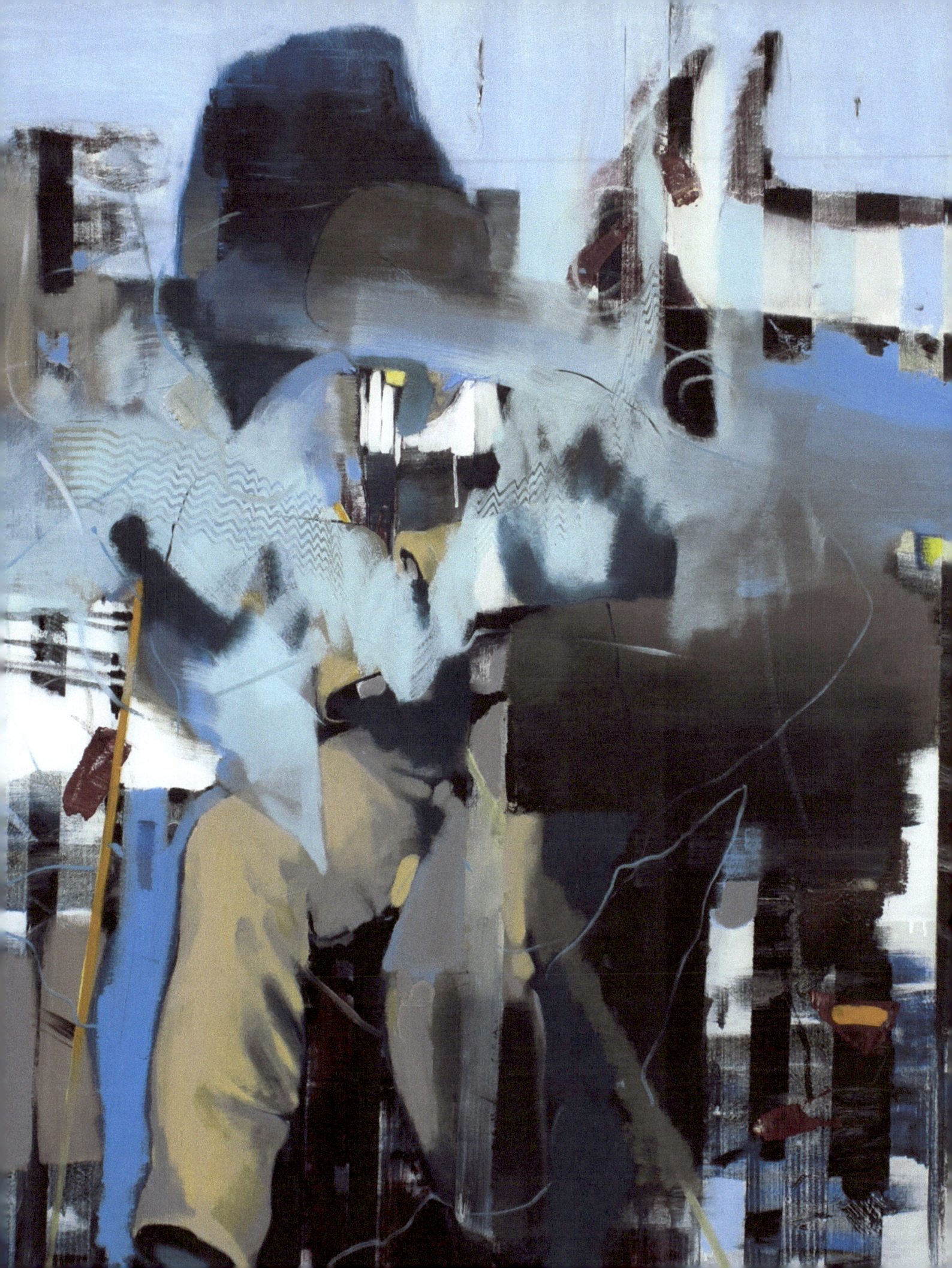

Francis Bacon Chair

oil on canvas

155x125

2016

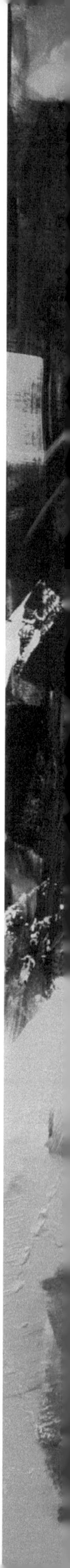

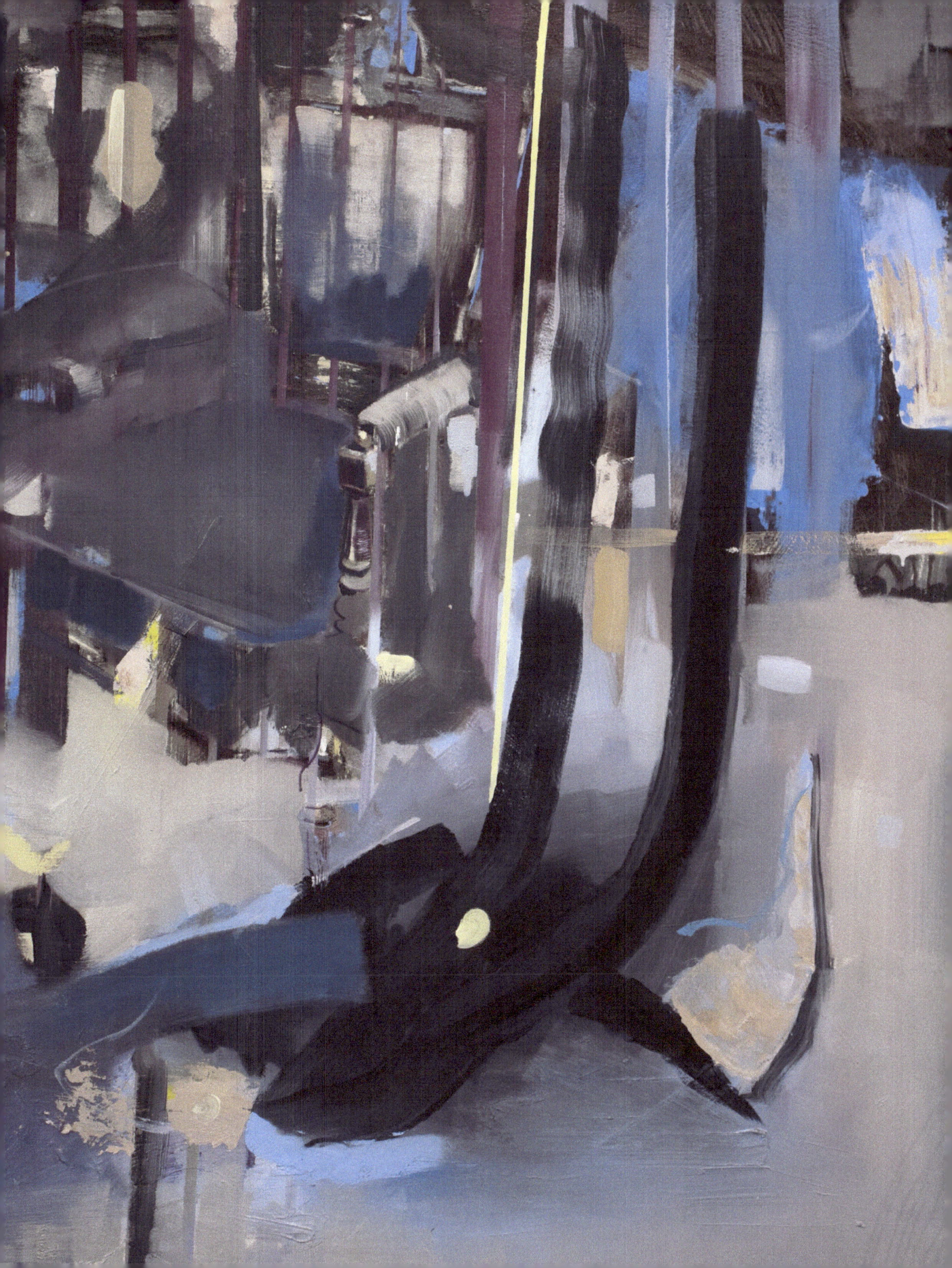

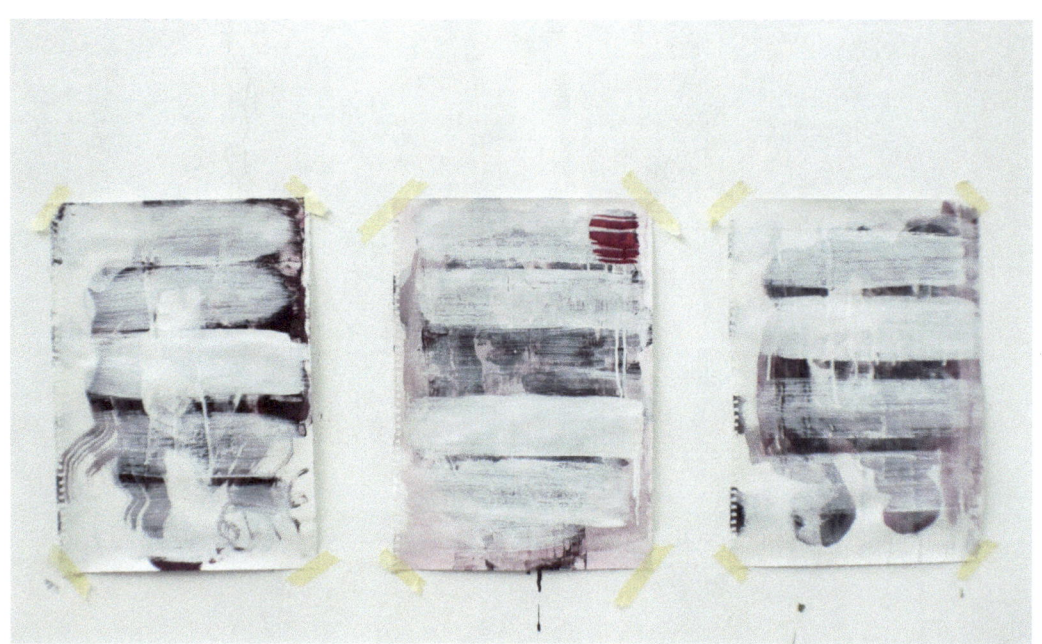

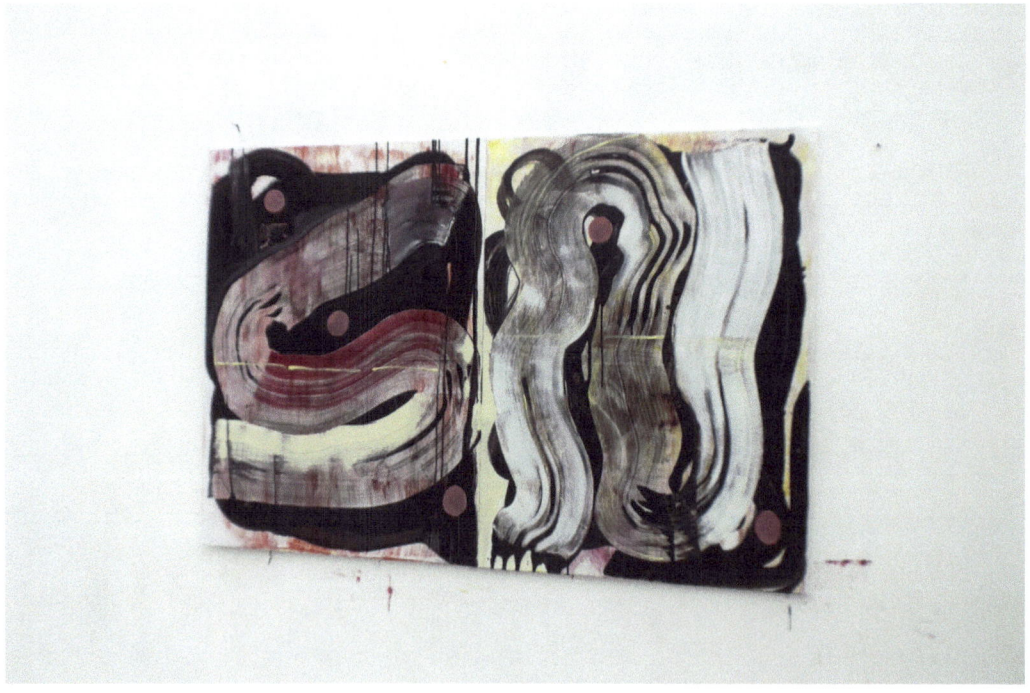

Recollections

oil on canvas

127x127cm

2016

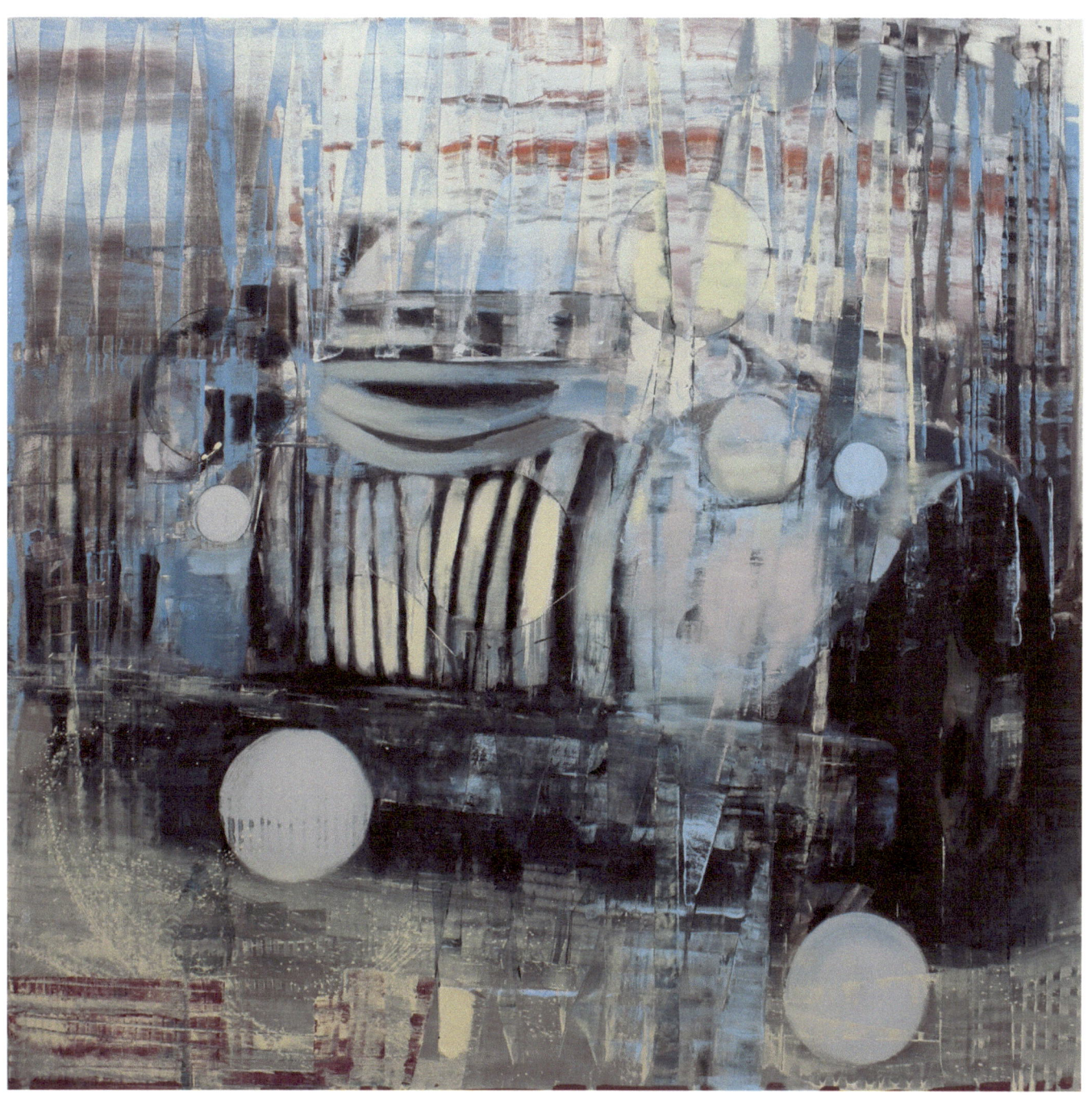

Choice Compilation I

oil on canvas

157127cm

2016

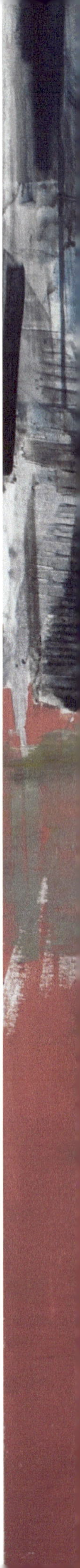

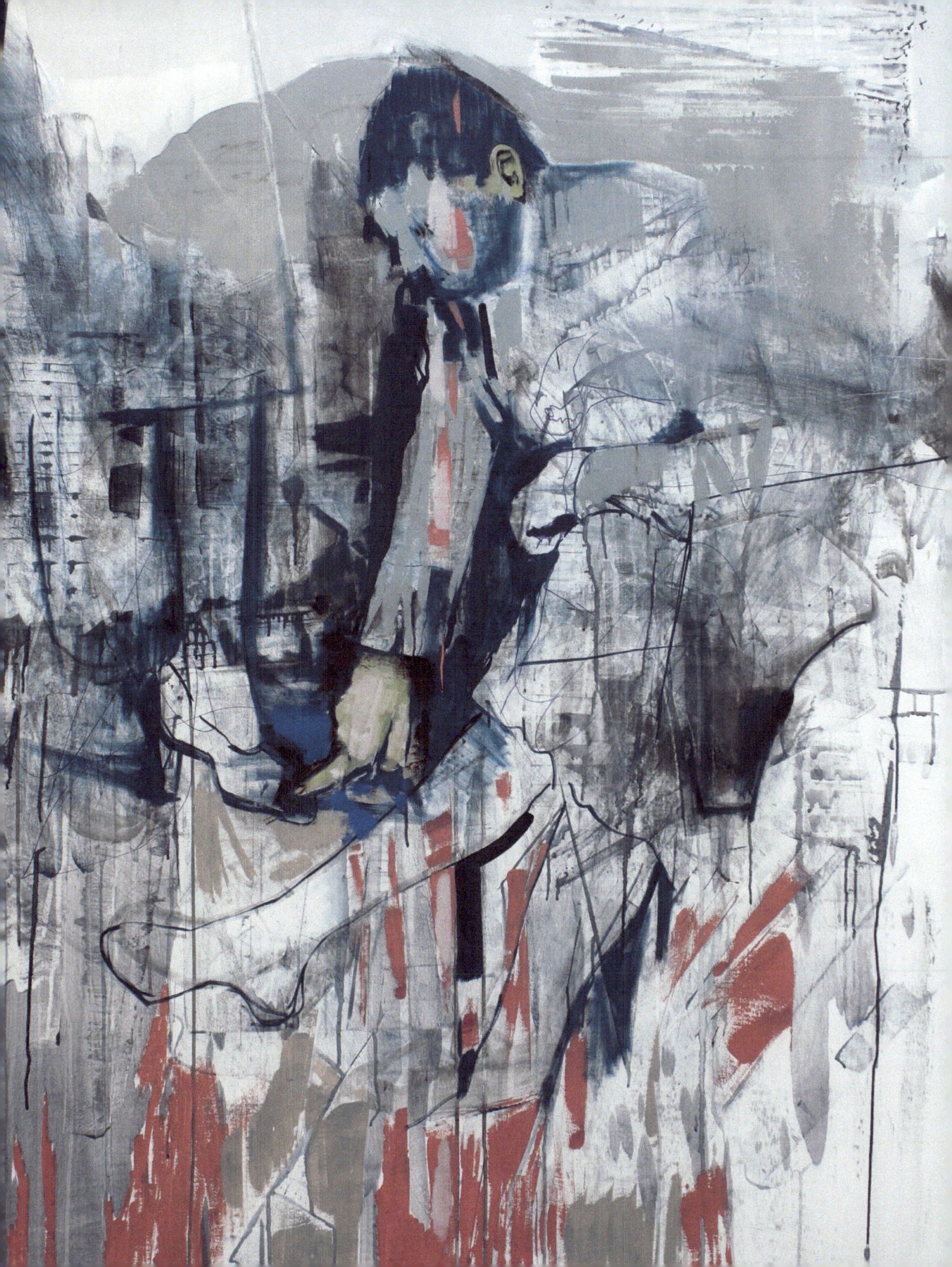

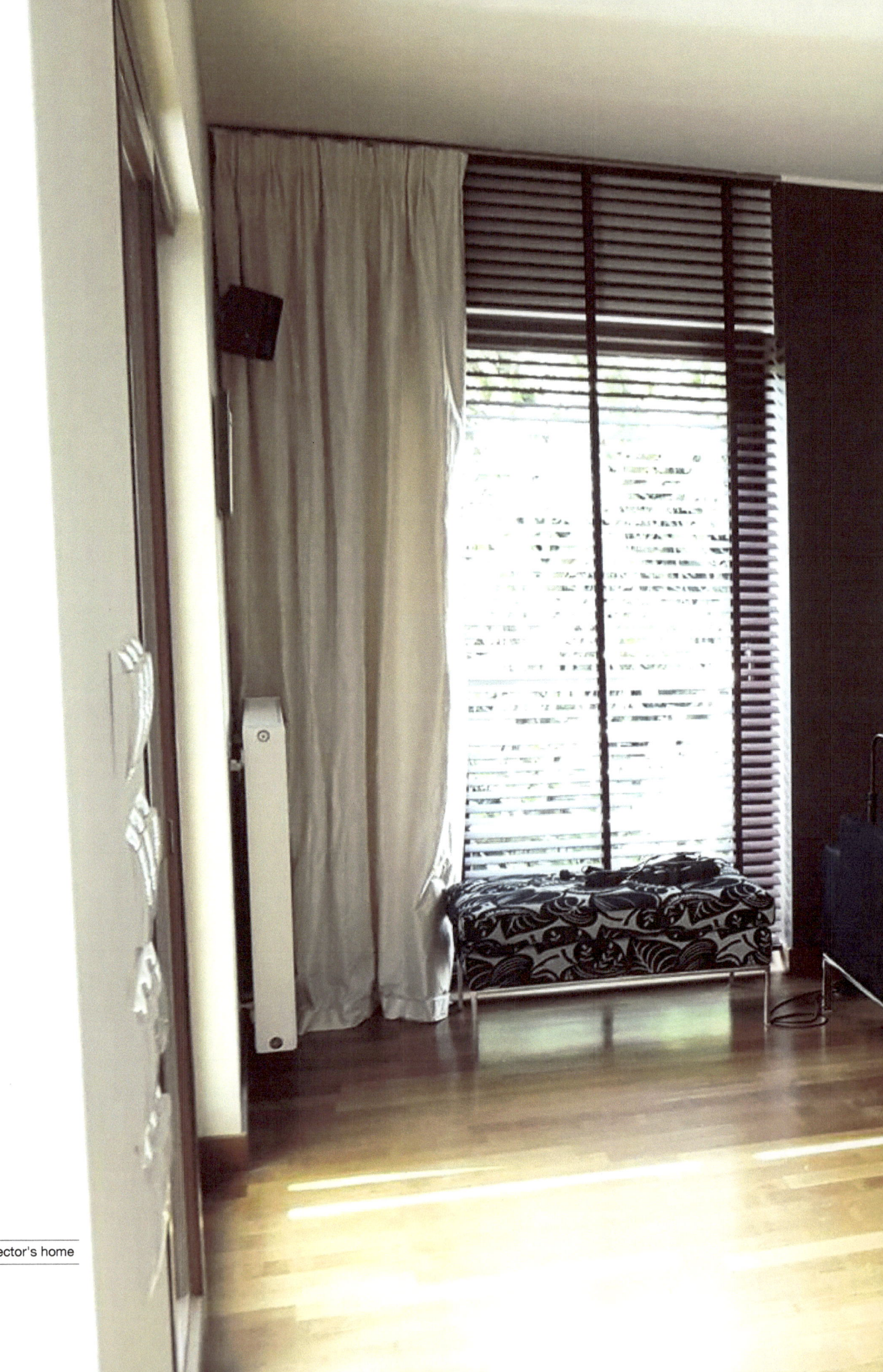

Man in Blue

work at a collector's home

2016

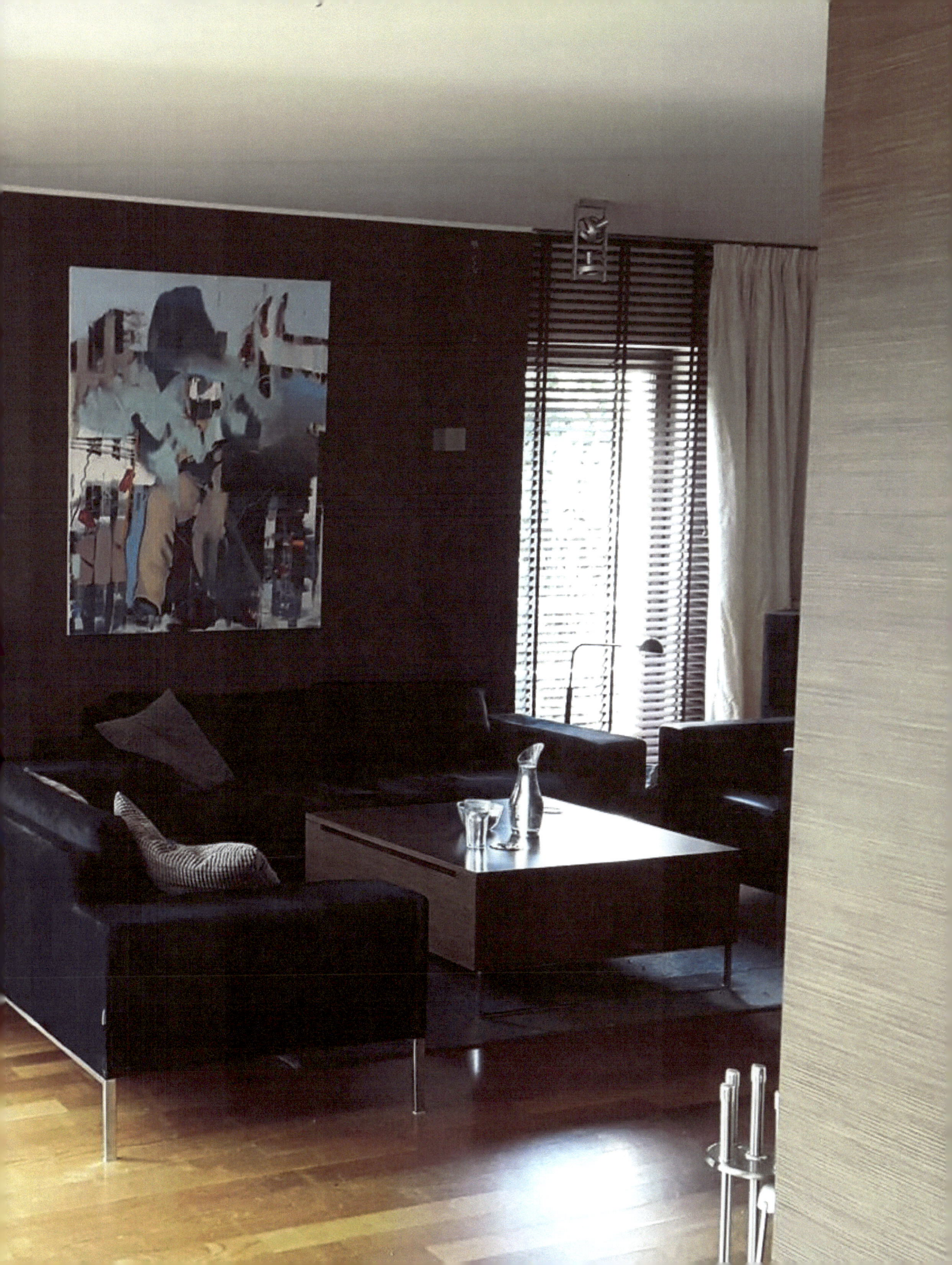

Neither Twins Series

**Neither Sisters,
Neither Twins I**

oil on canvas

30x48cm

2016

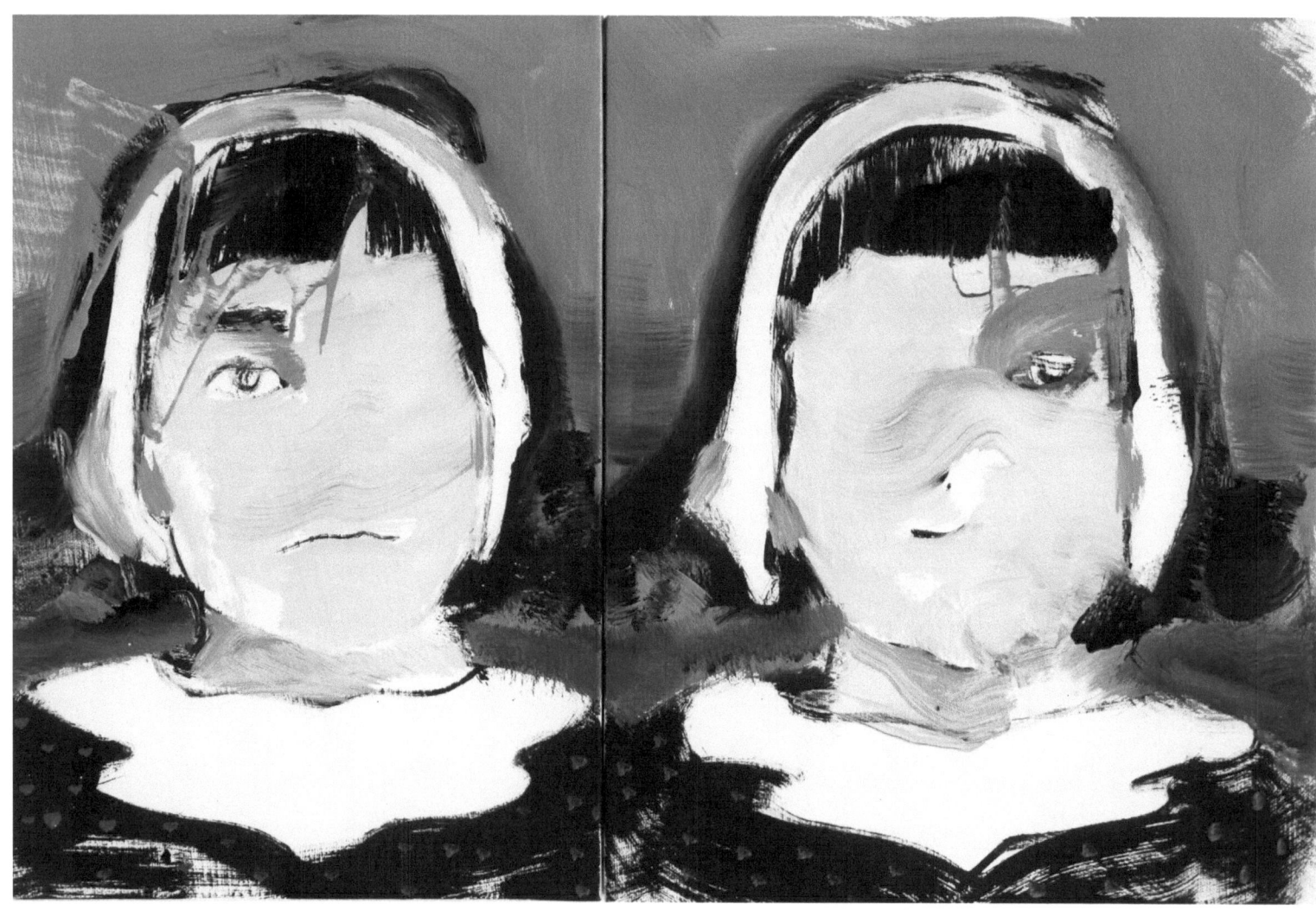

**Neither Sisters,
Neither Twins II**

oil on canvas

30x48cm

2016

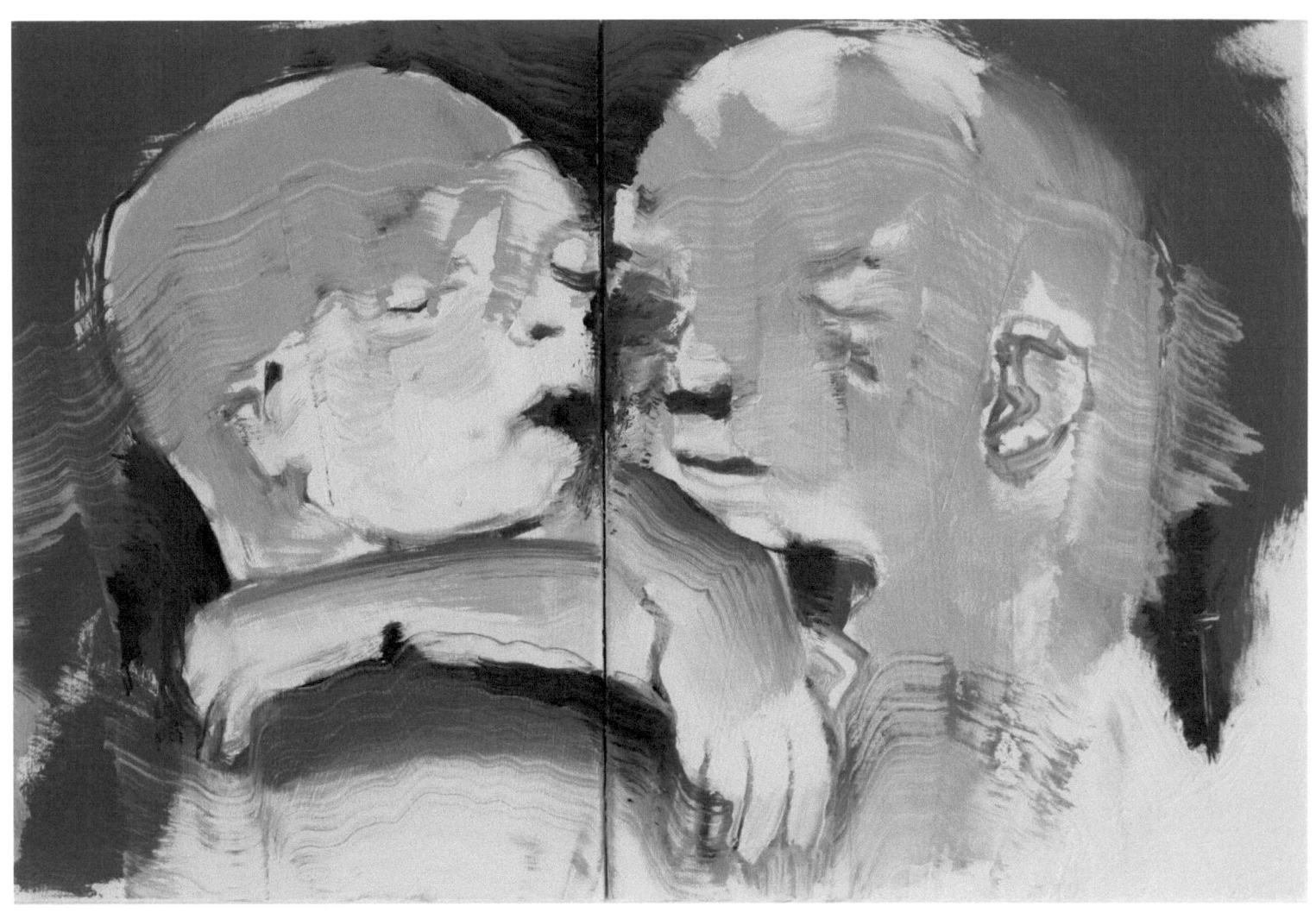

Neither Sisters,
Neither Twins IV

oil on canvas

38x48cm

2016

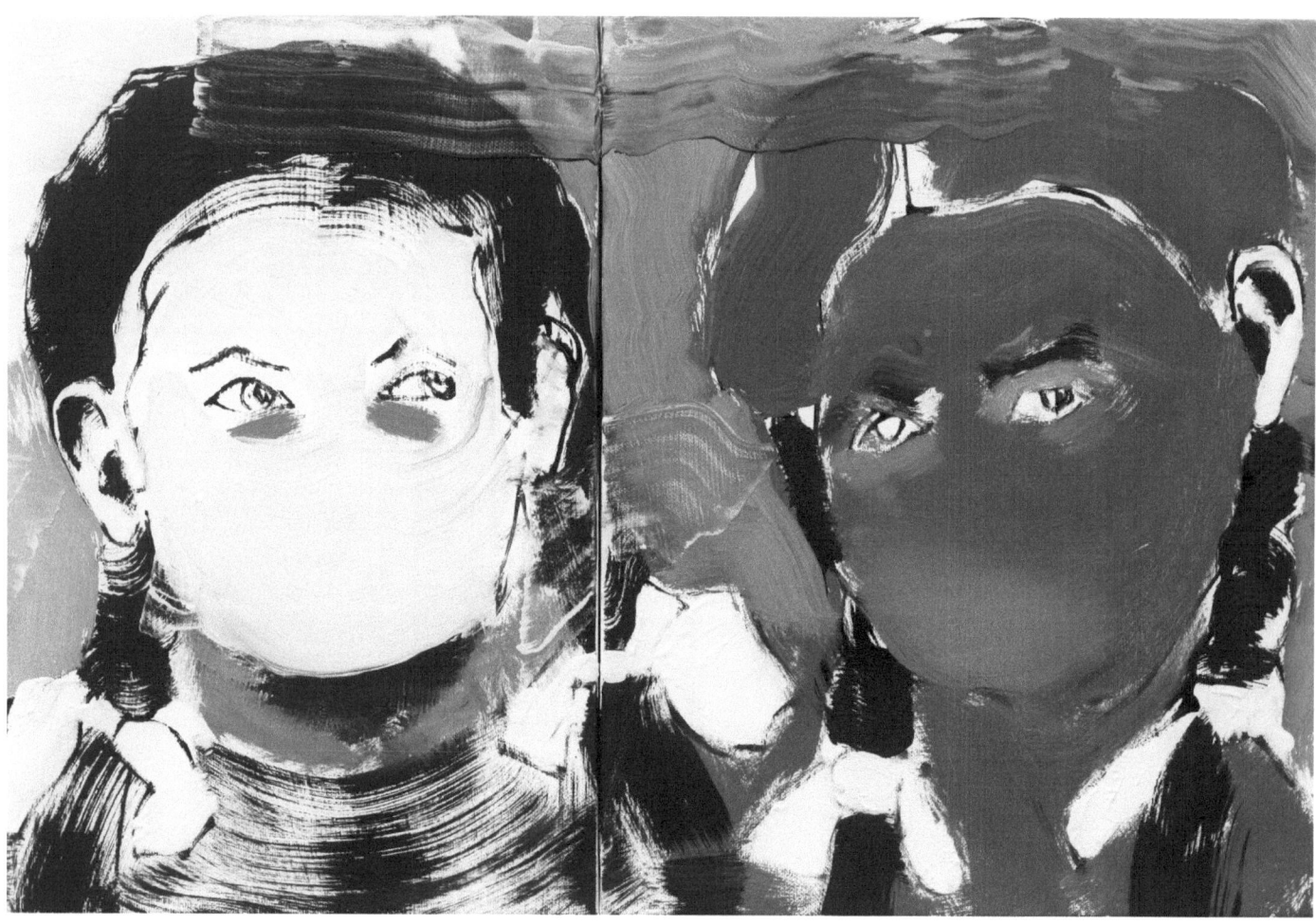

**Neither Brothers,
Neither Twins**

oil on canvas

150x200cm

2016

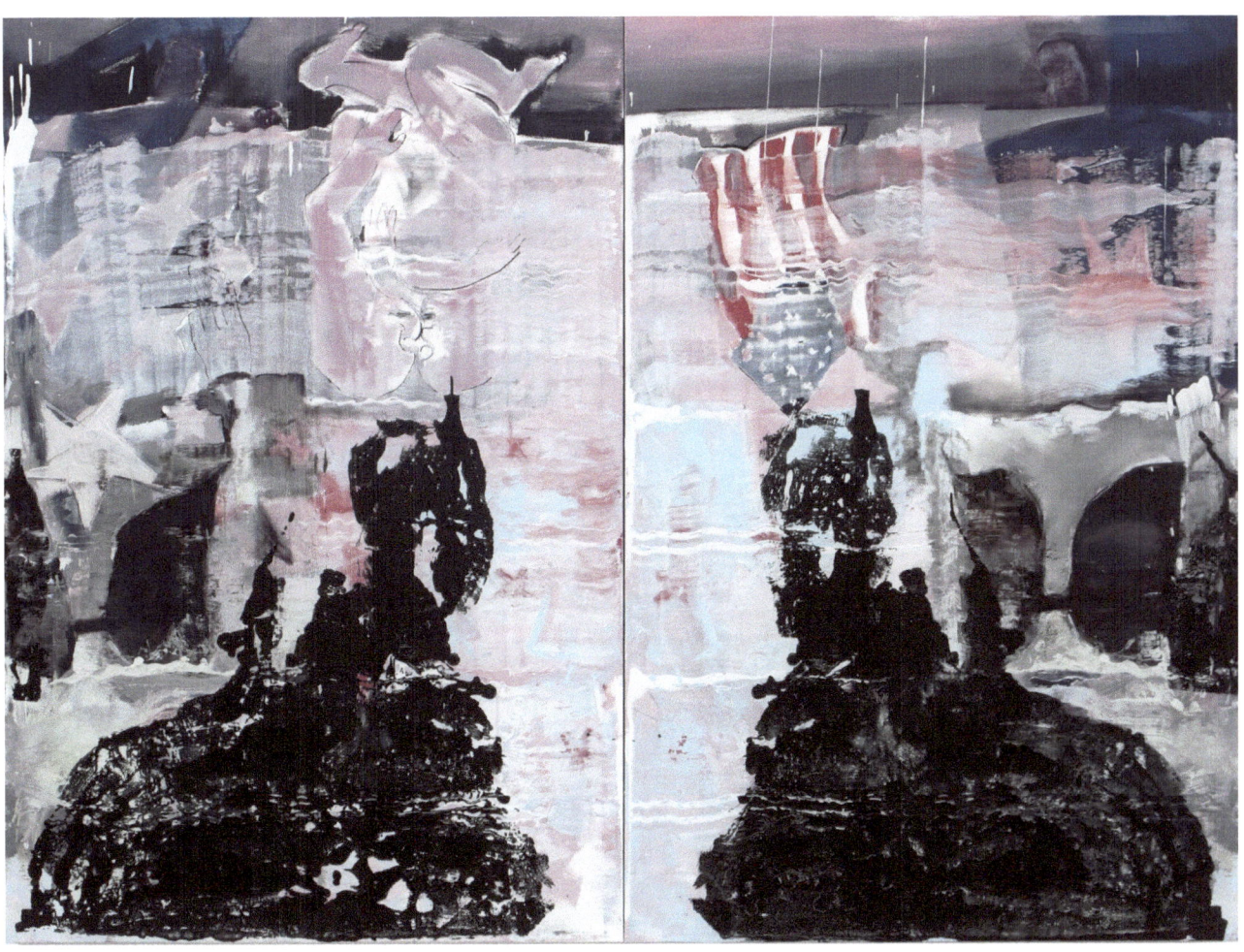

**Neither Sisters,
Neither Twins (Red) I**

oil on canvas

50x70cm

2016

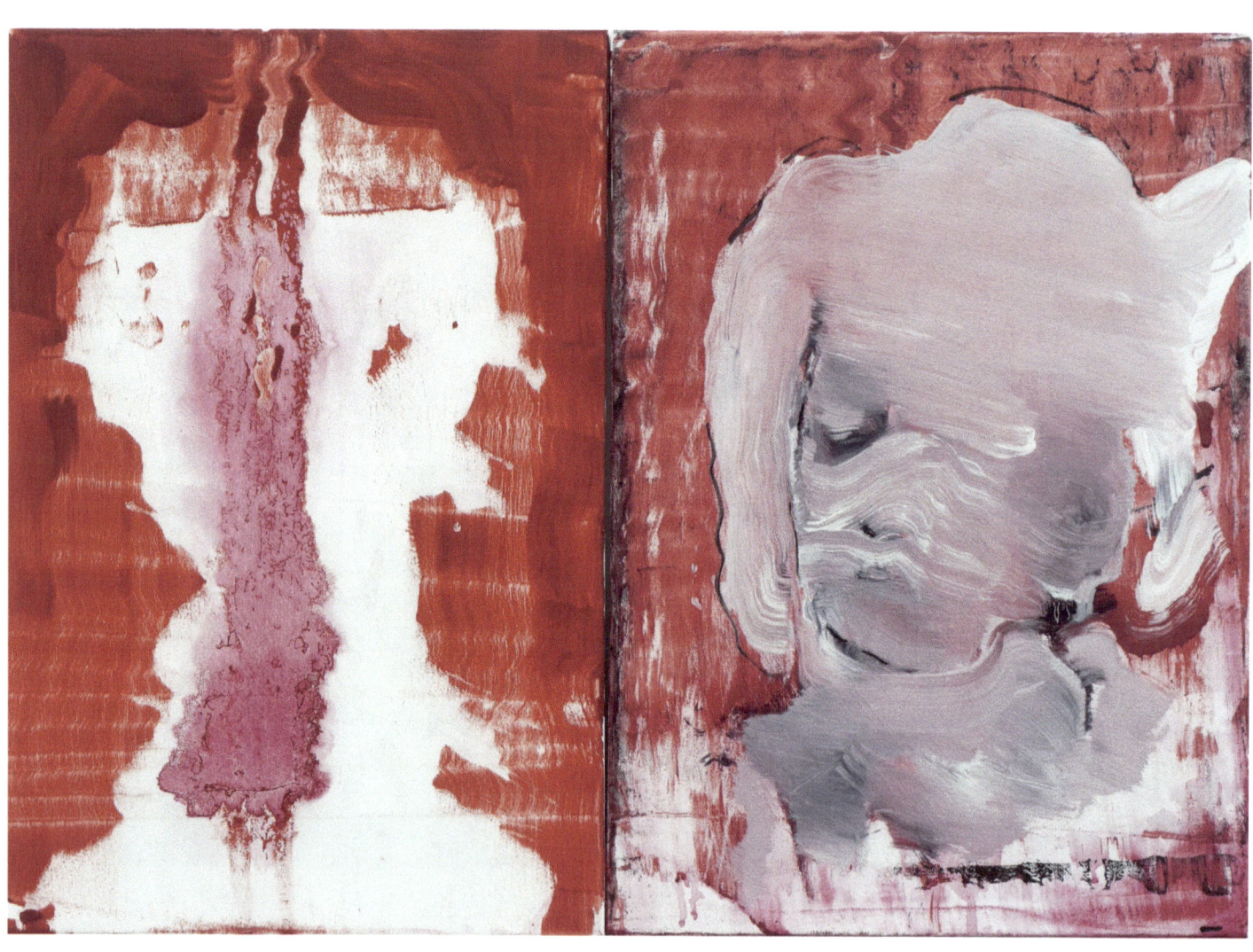

Neither Sisters,
Neither Twins (Red) II

oil on canvas

50x70cm

2016

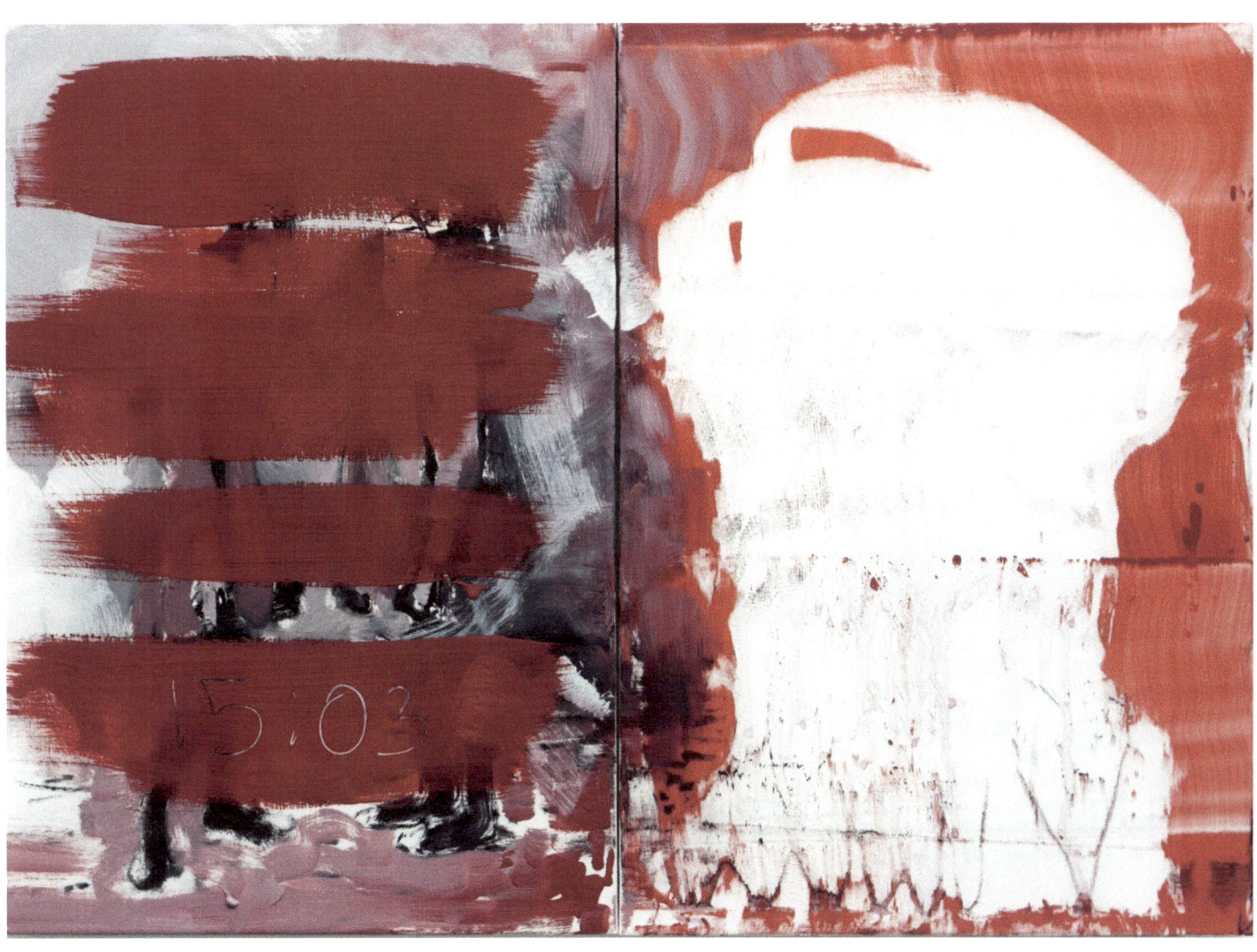

**Neither Brothers,
Neither Twins III**

oil on canvas

38x48cm

2016

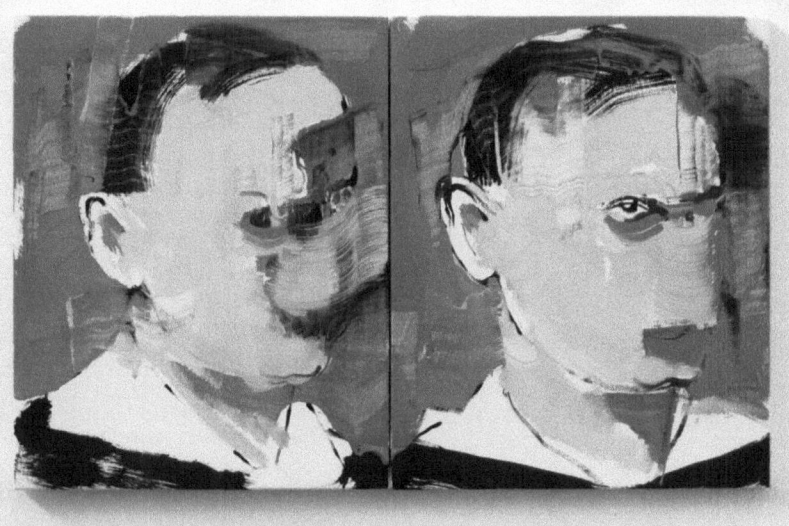

Neither Sisters,
Neither Twins V

oil on canvas

50x70cm

2016

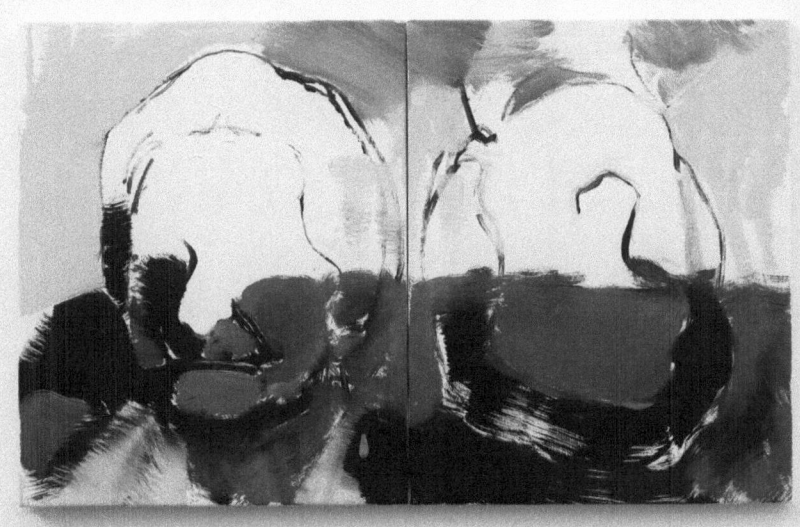

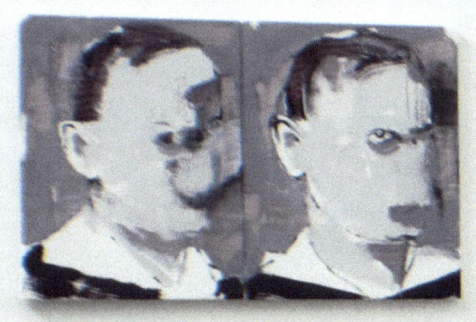

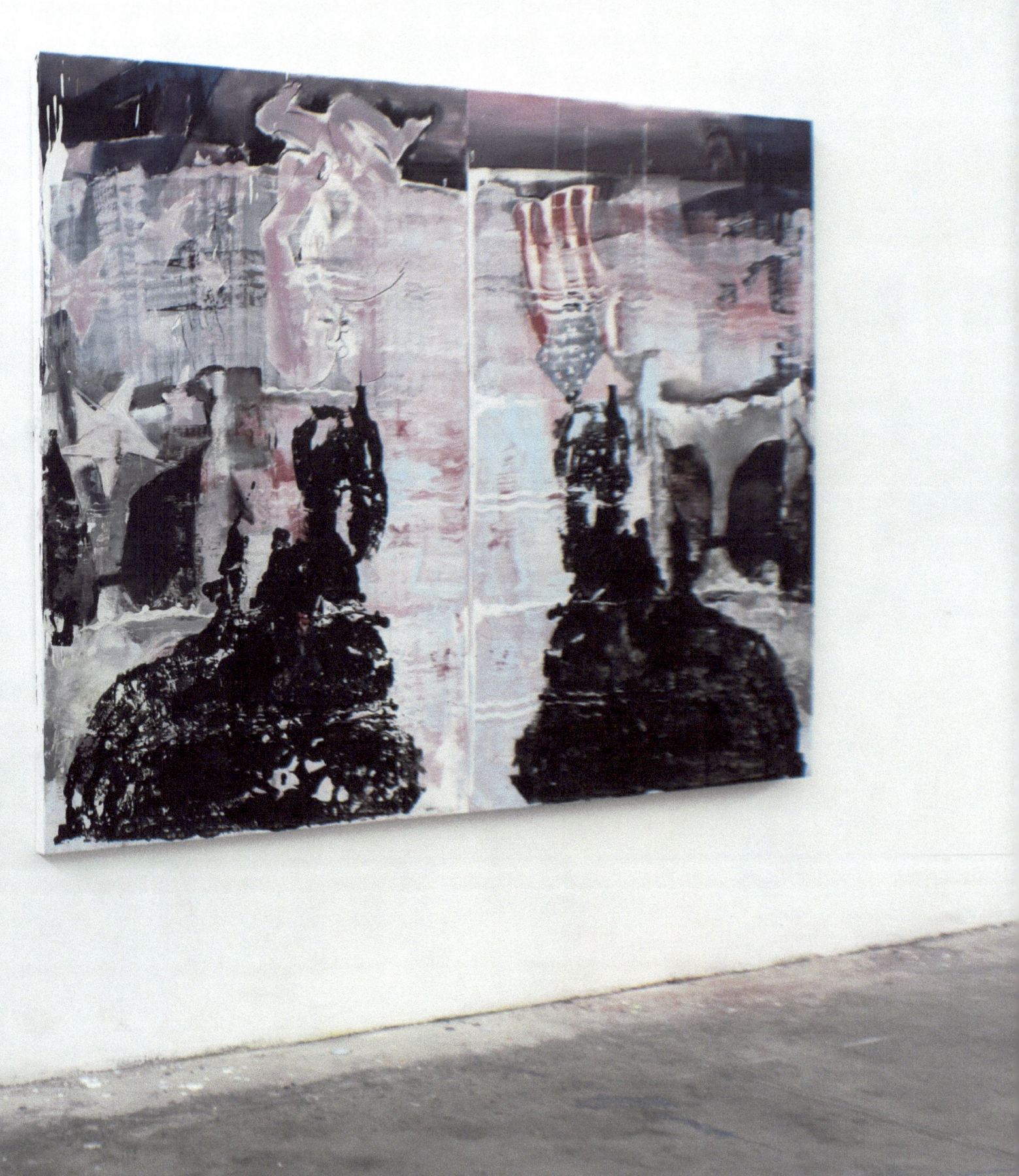

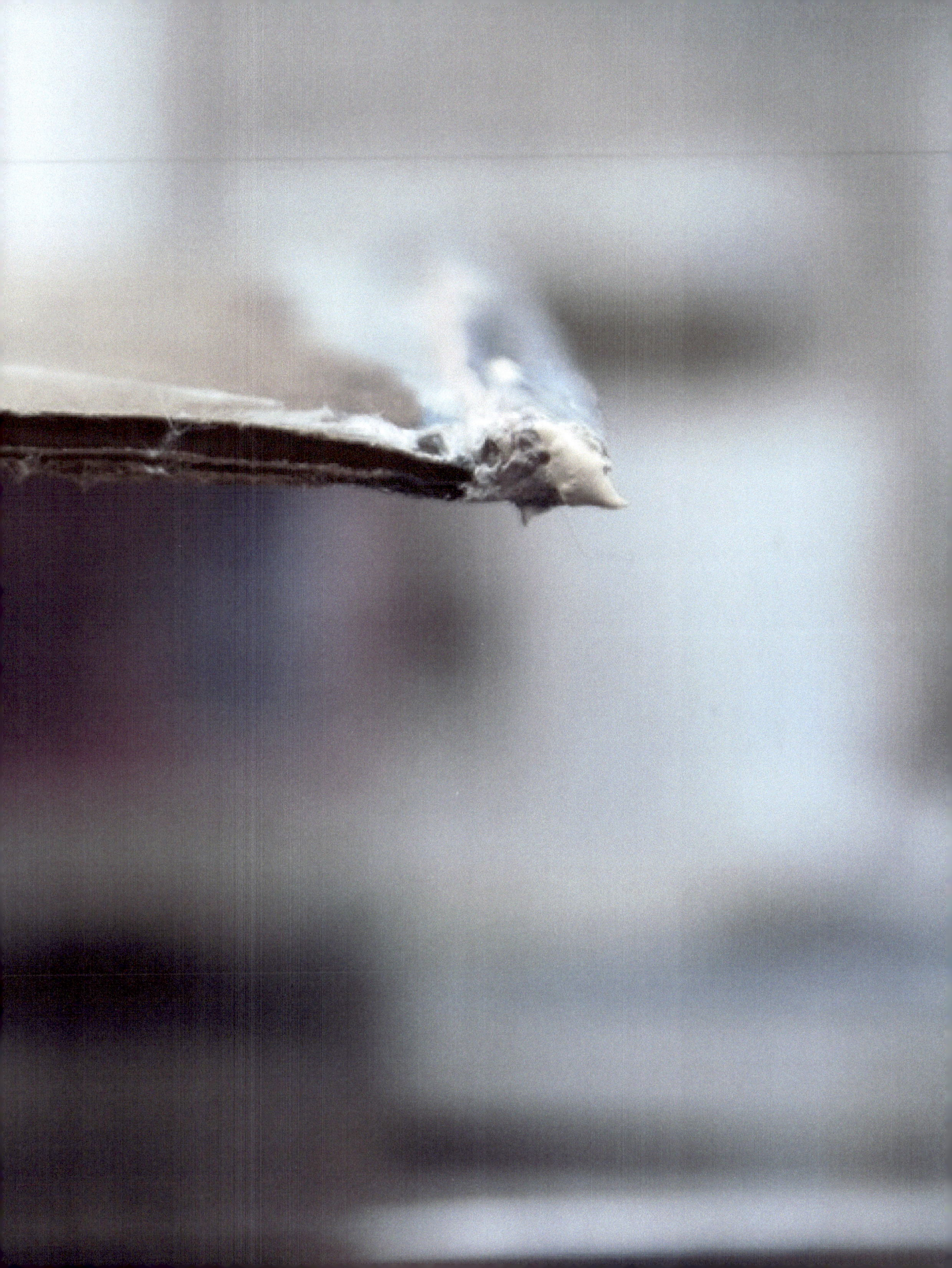

Studio
Pictures

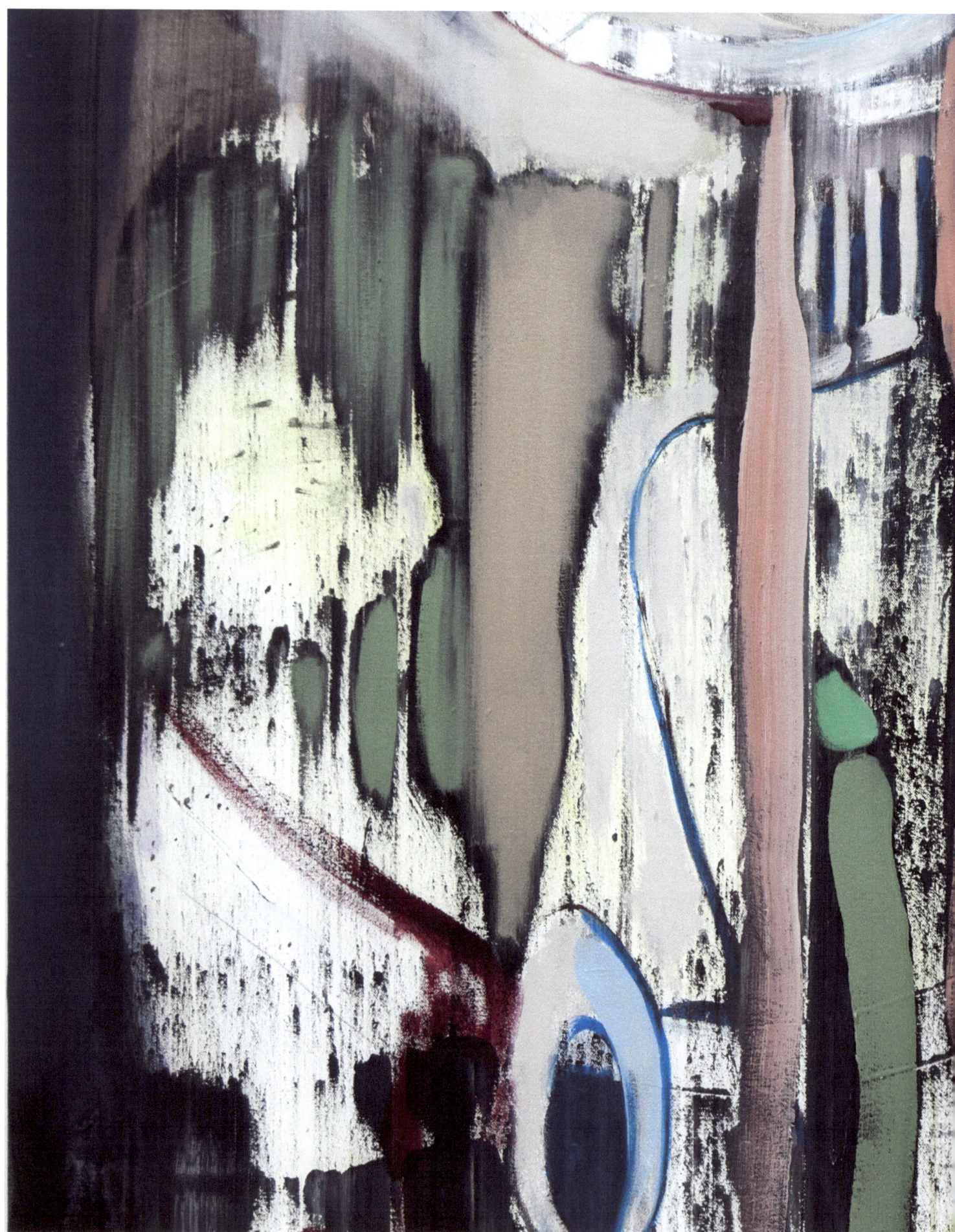

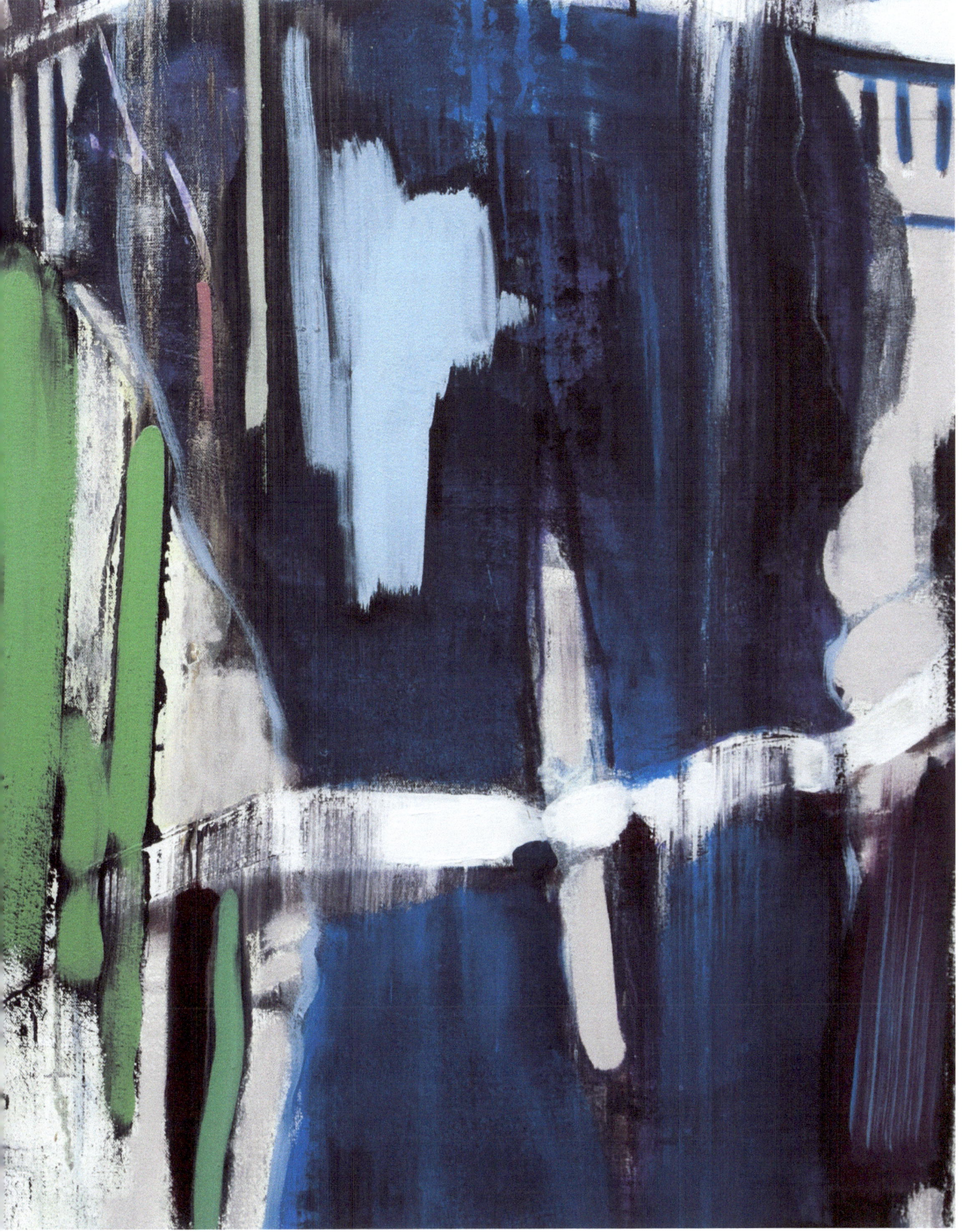

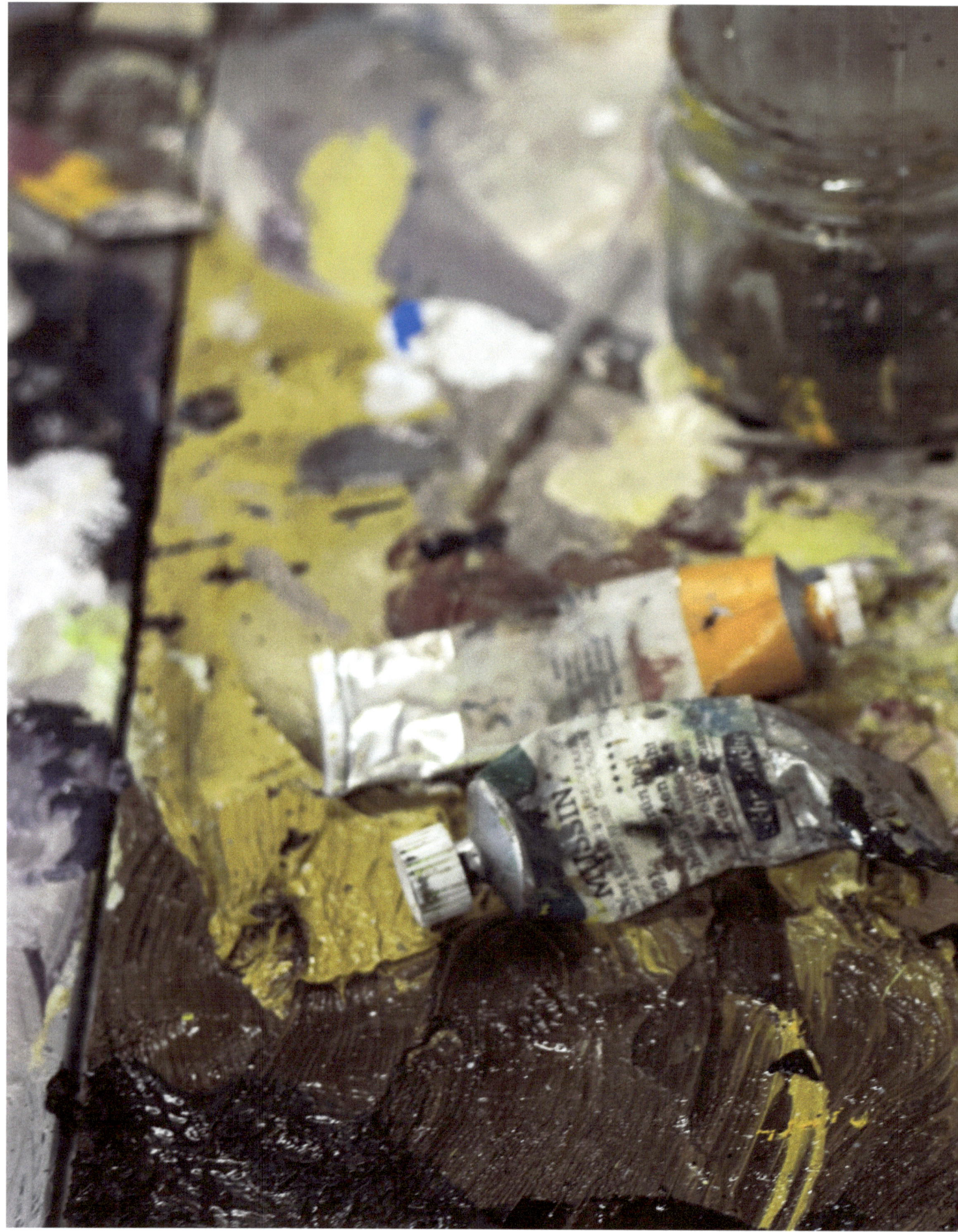

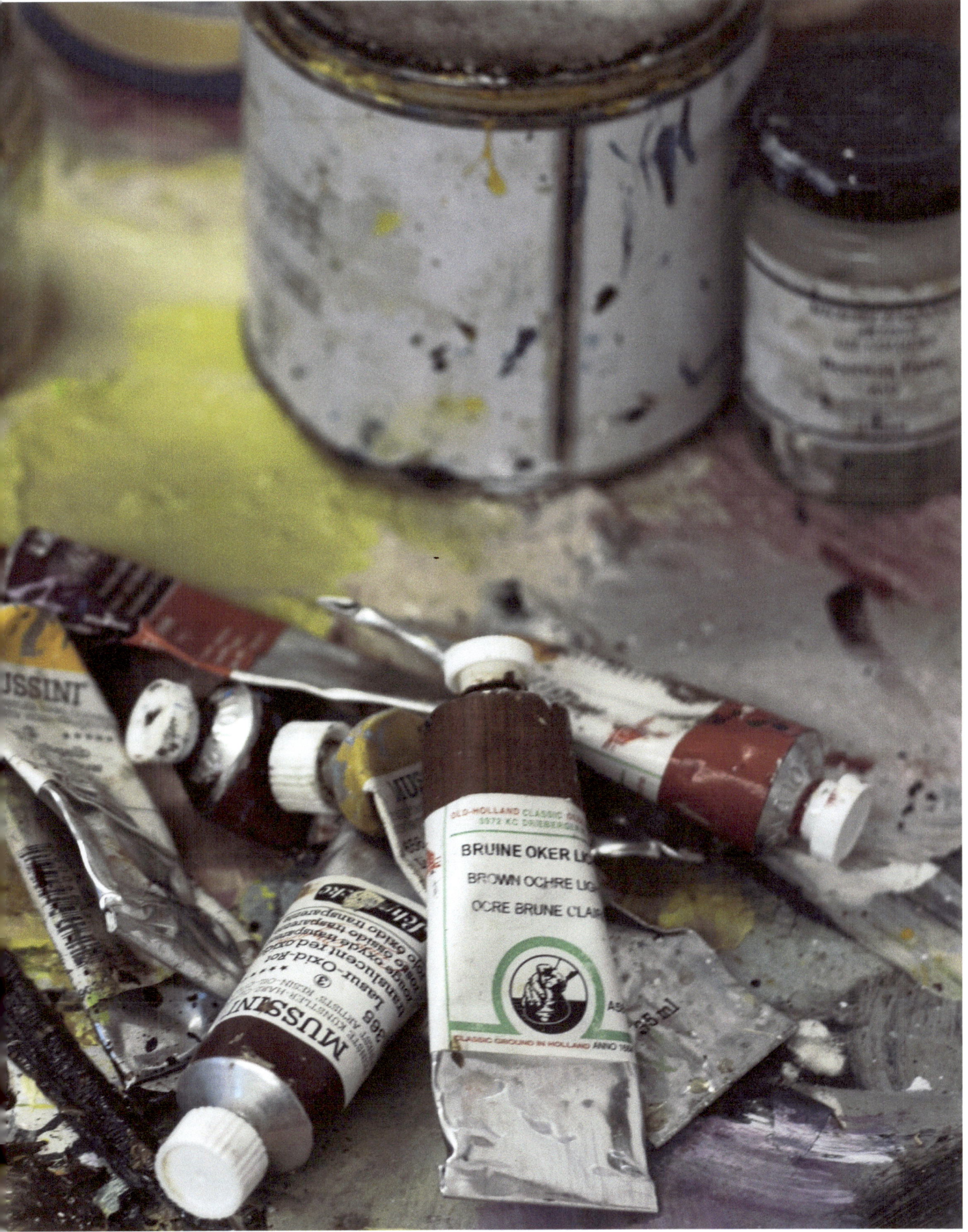

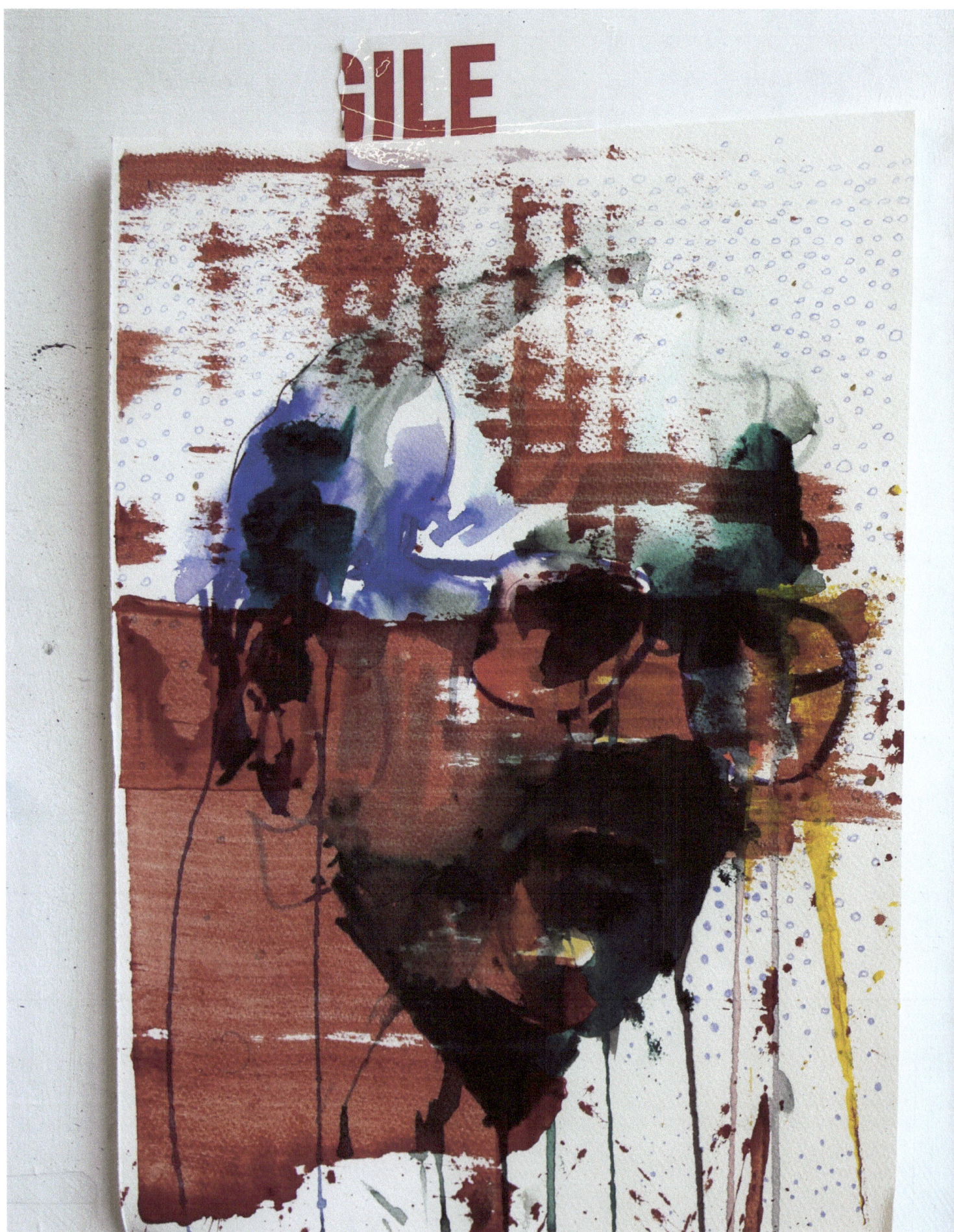

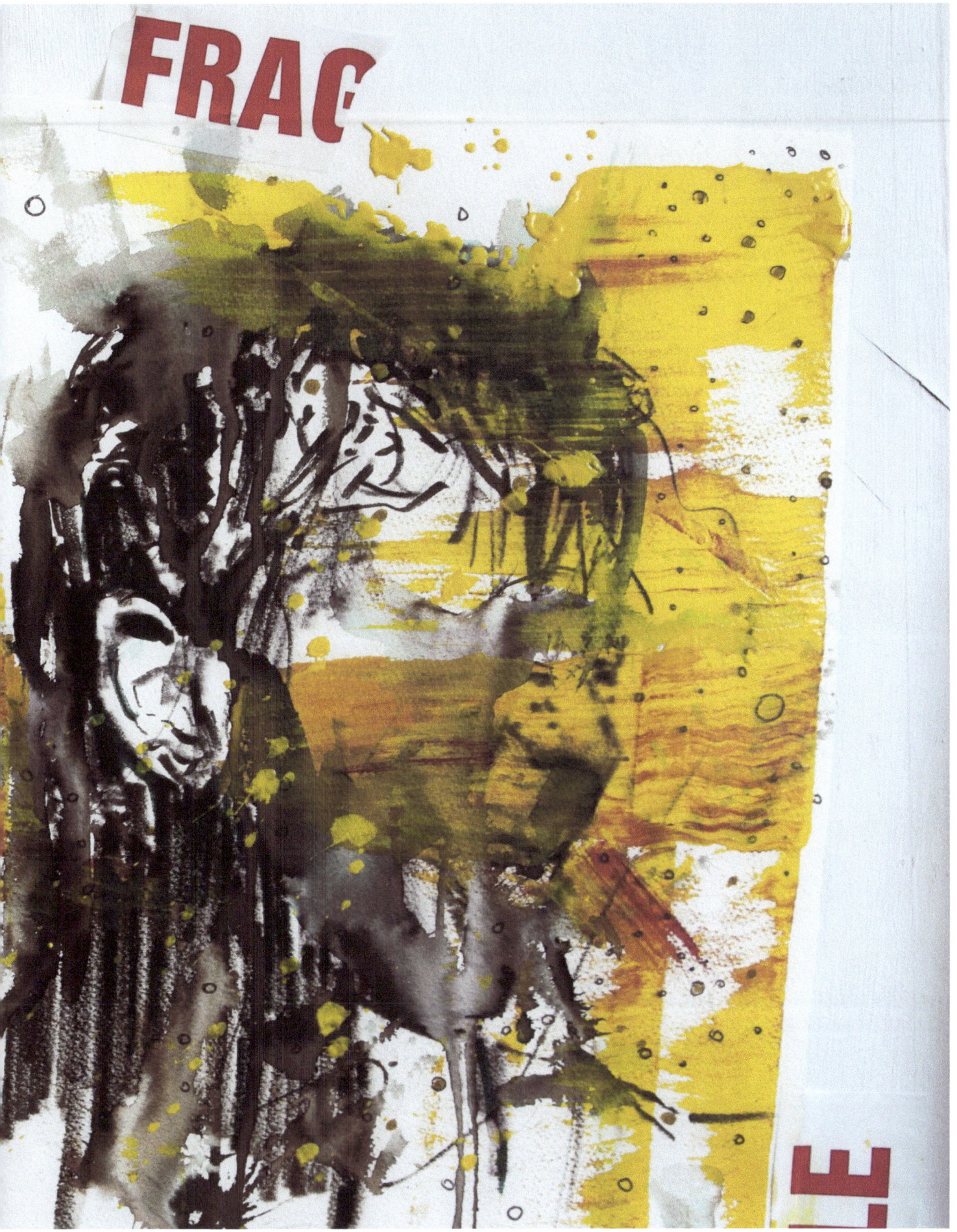

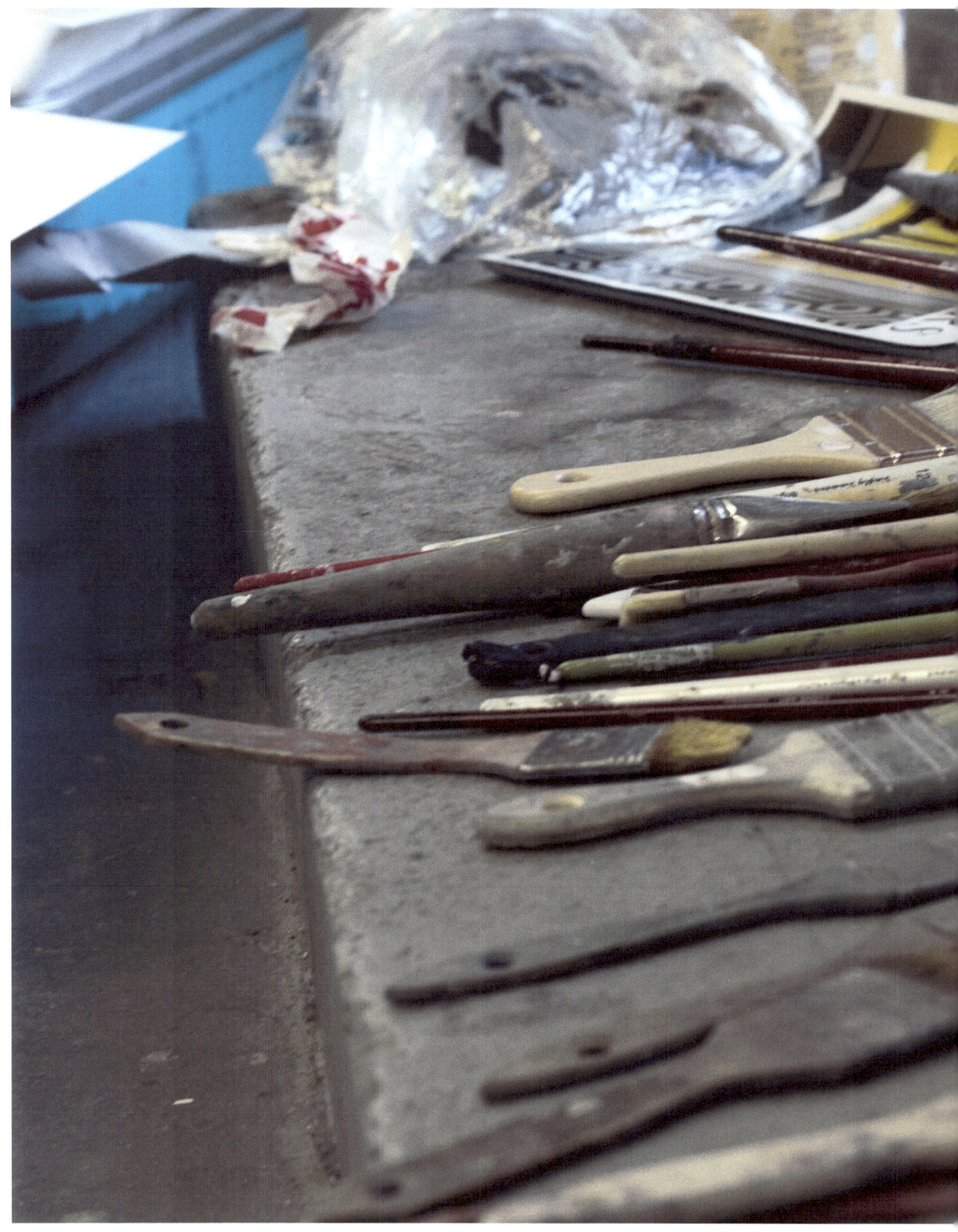

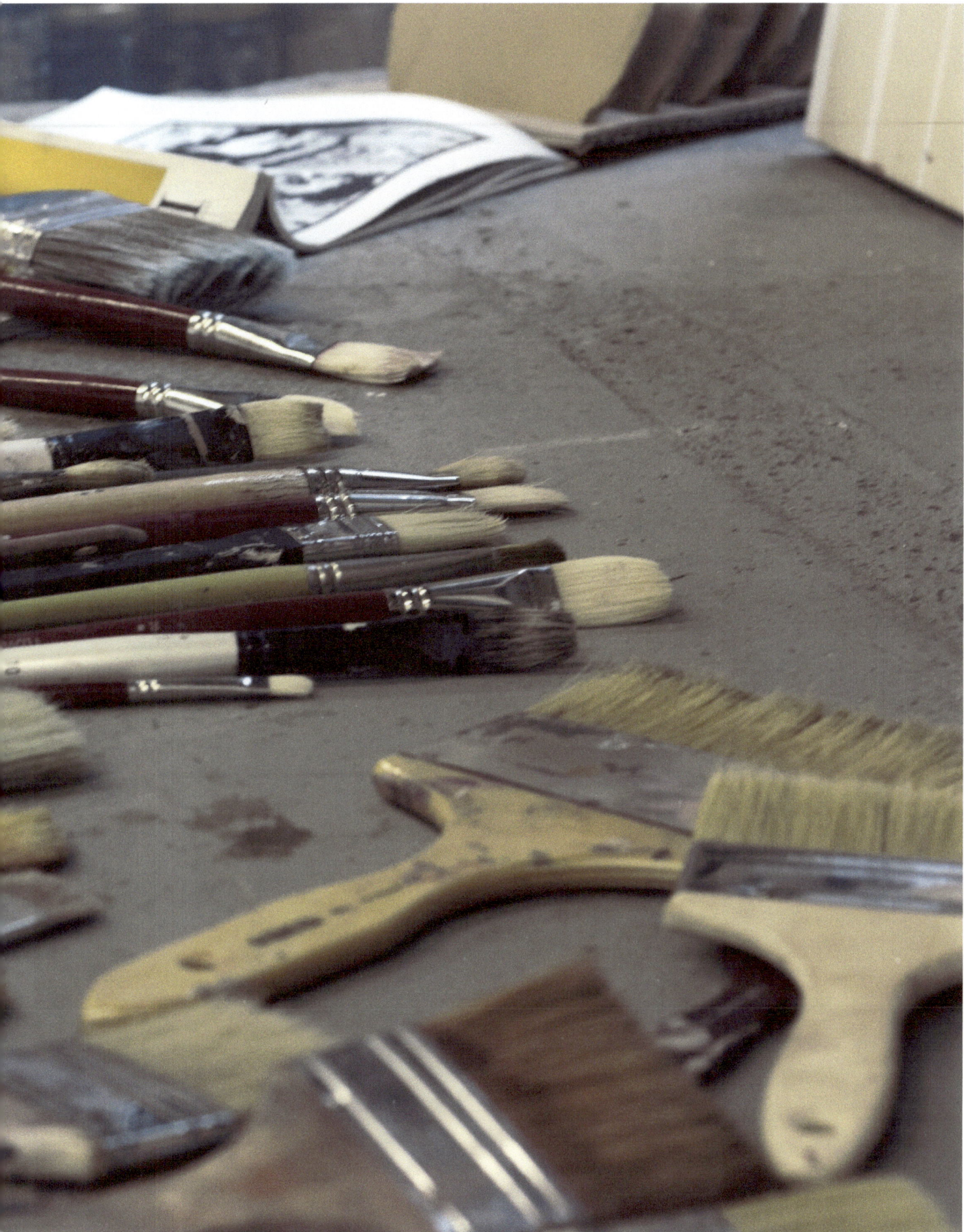

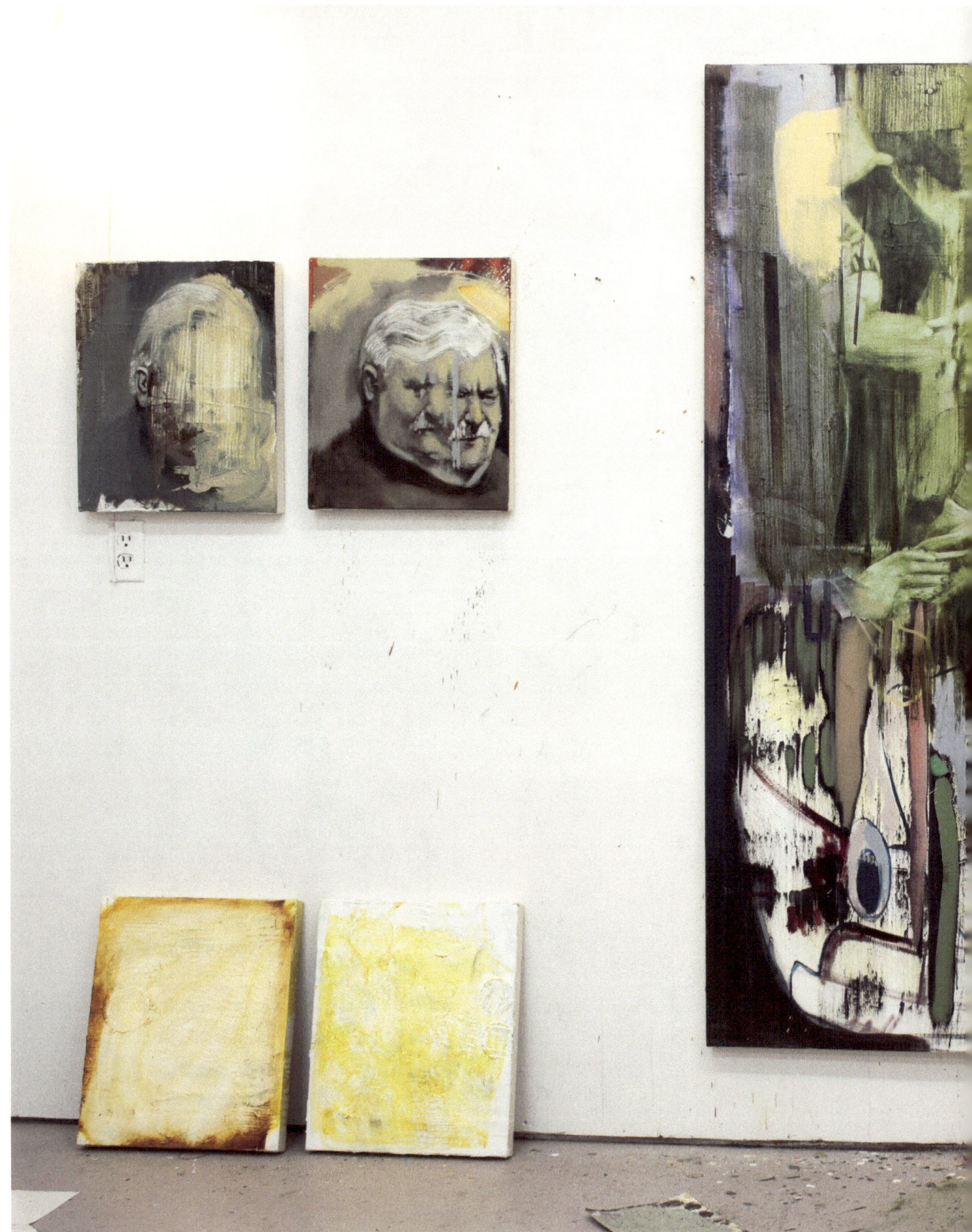

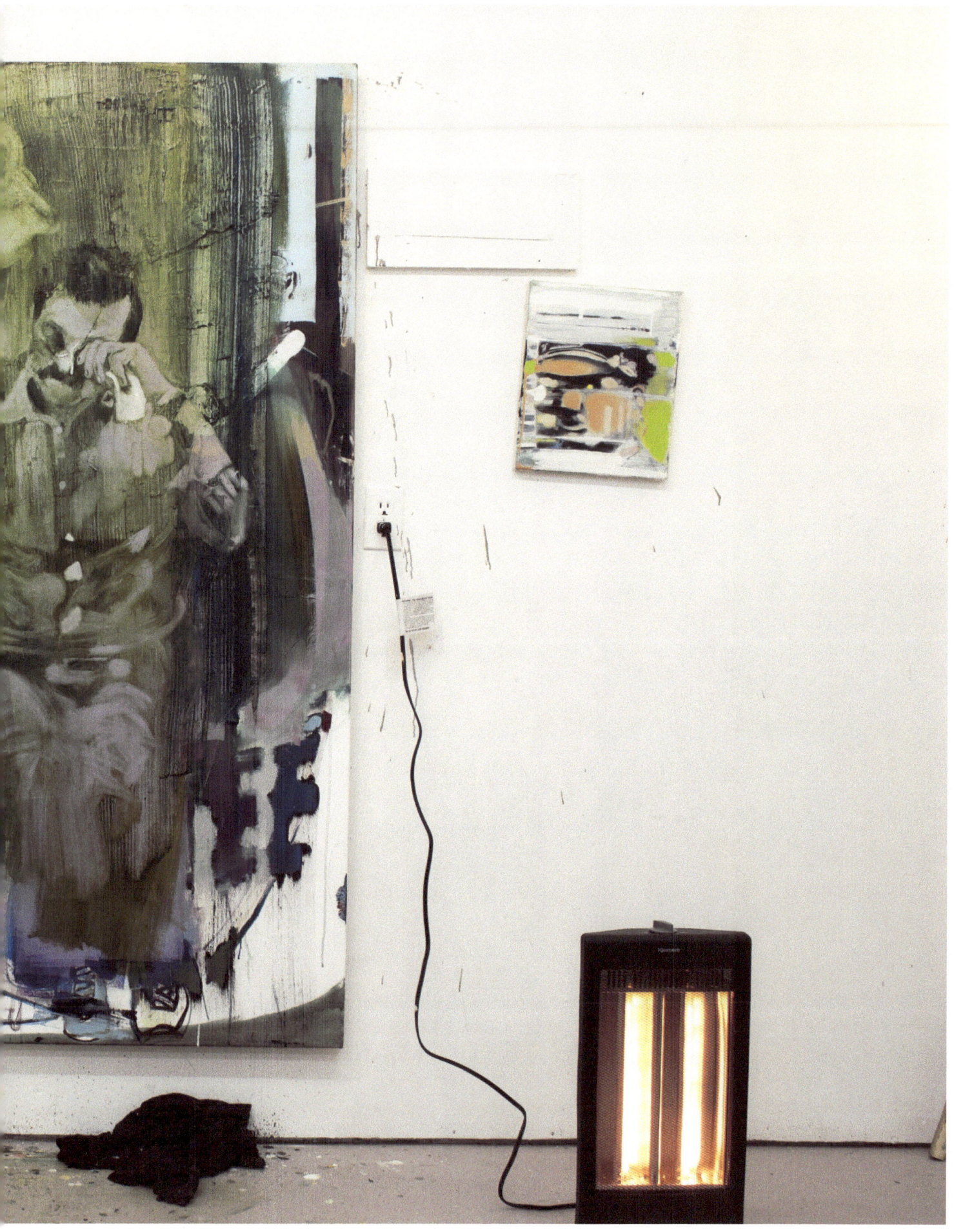

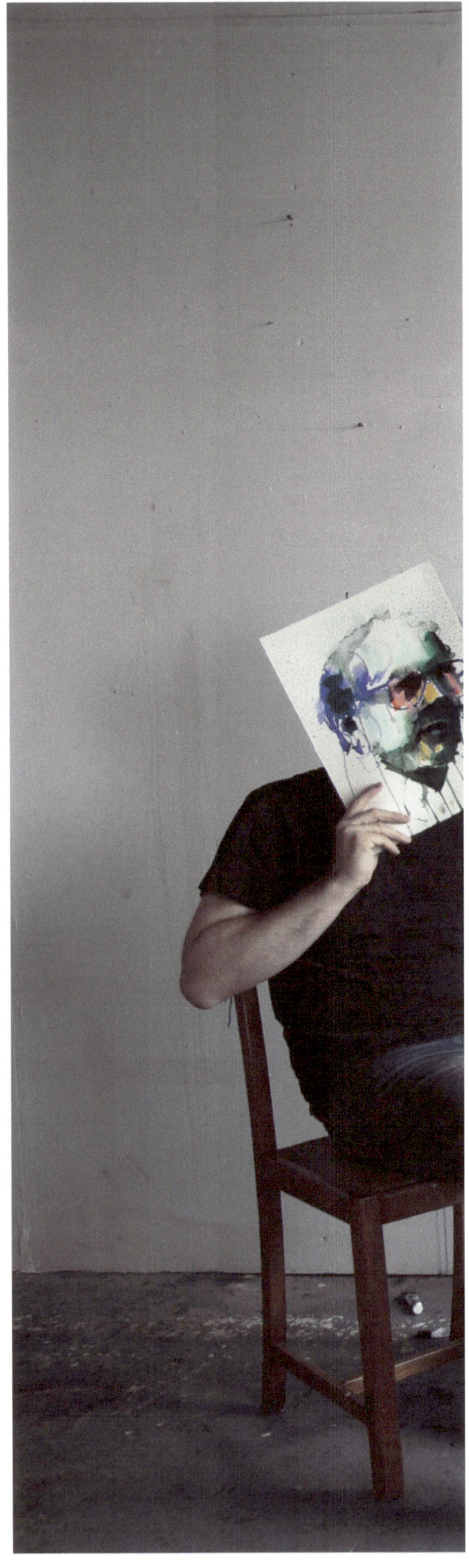
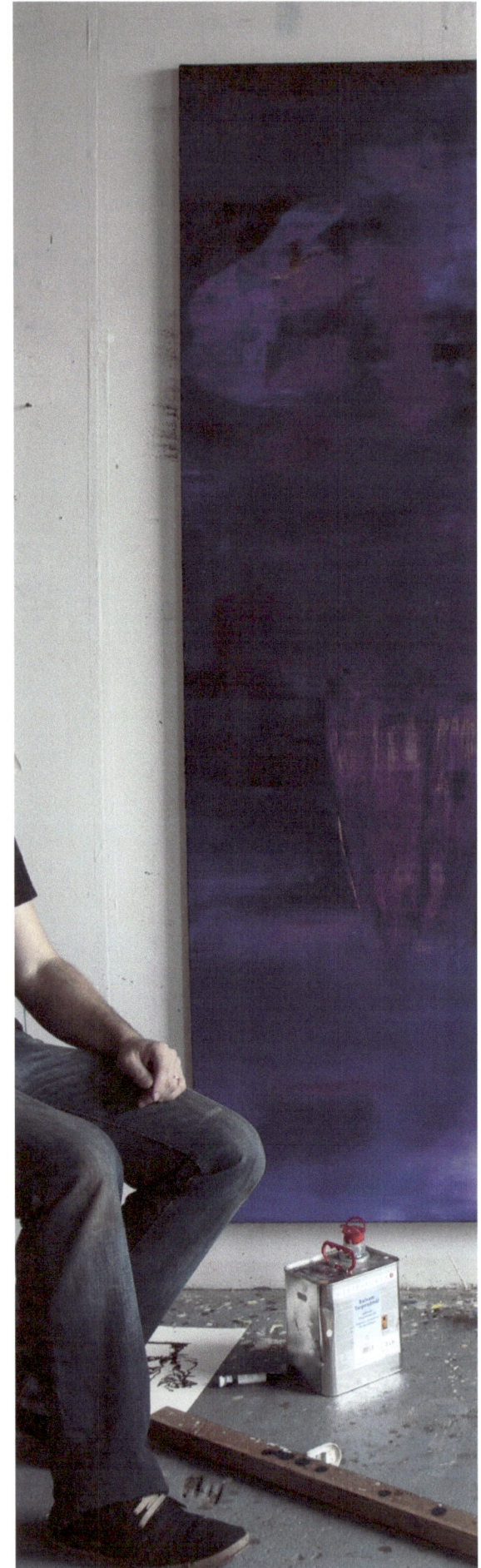
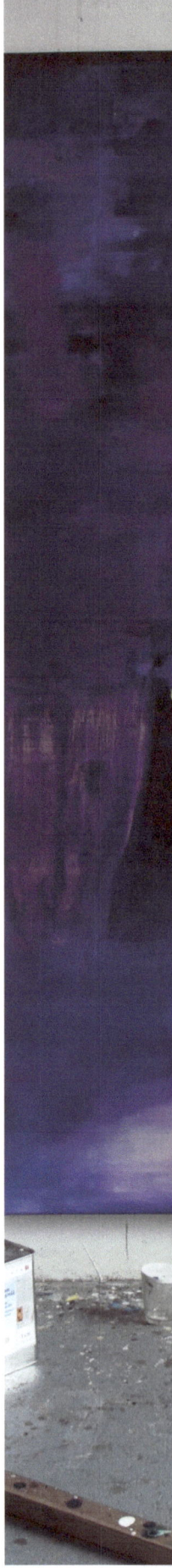

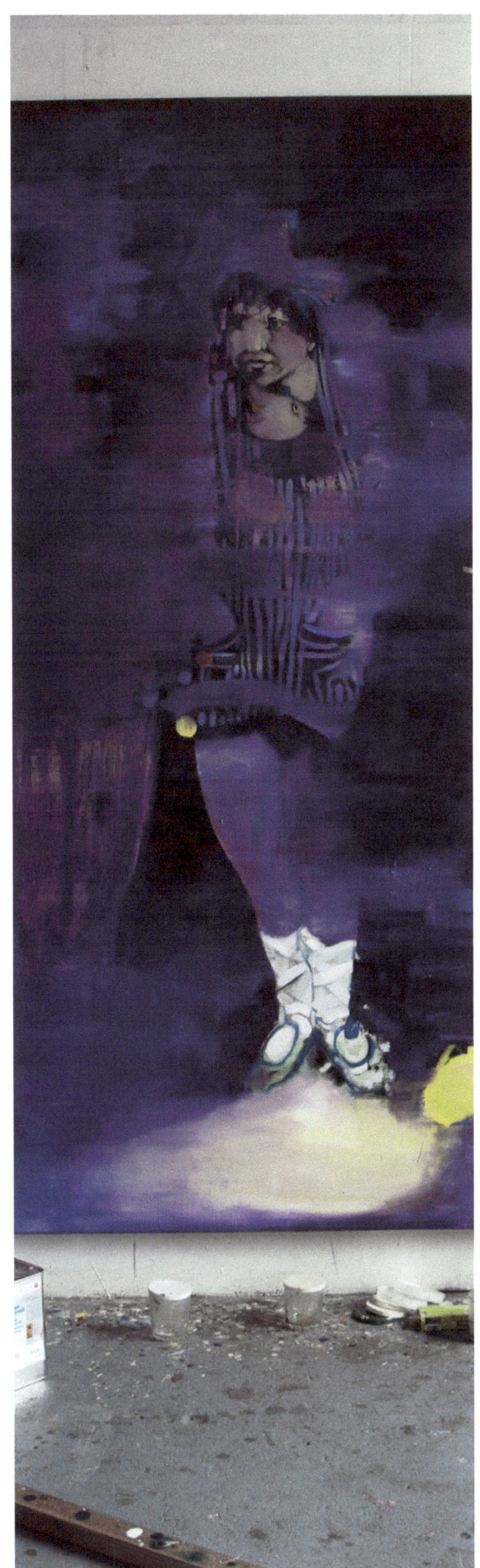
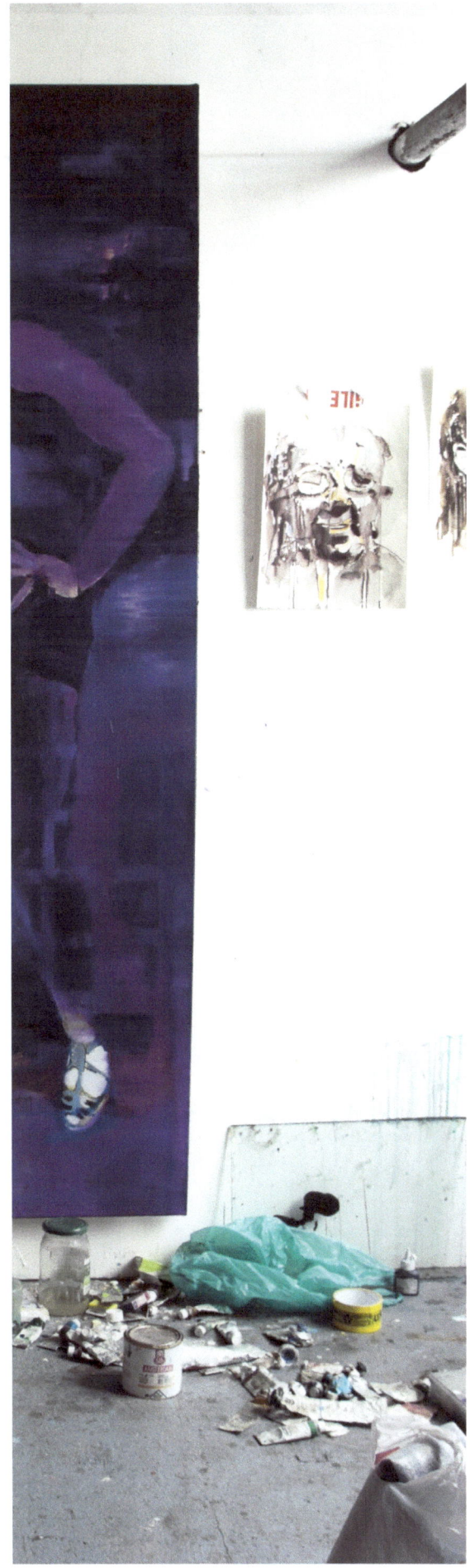

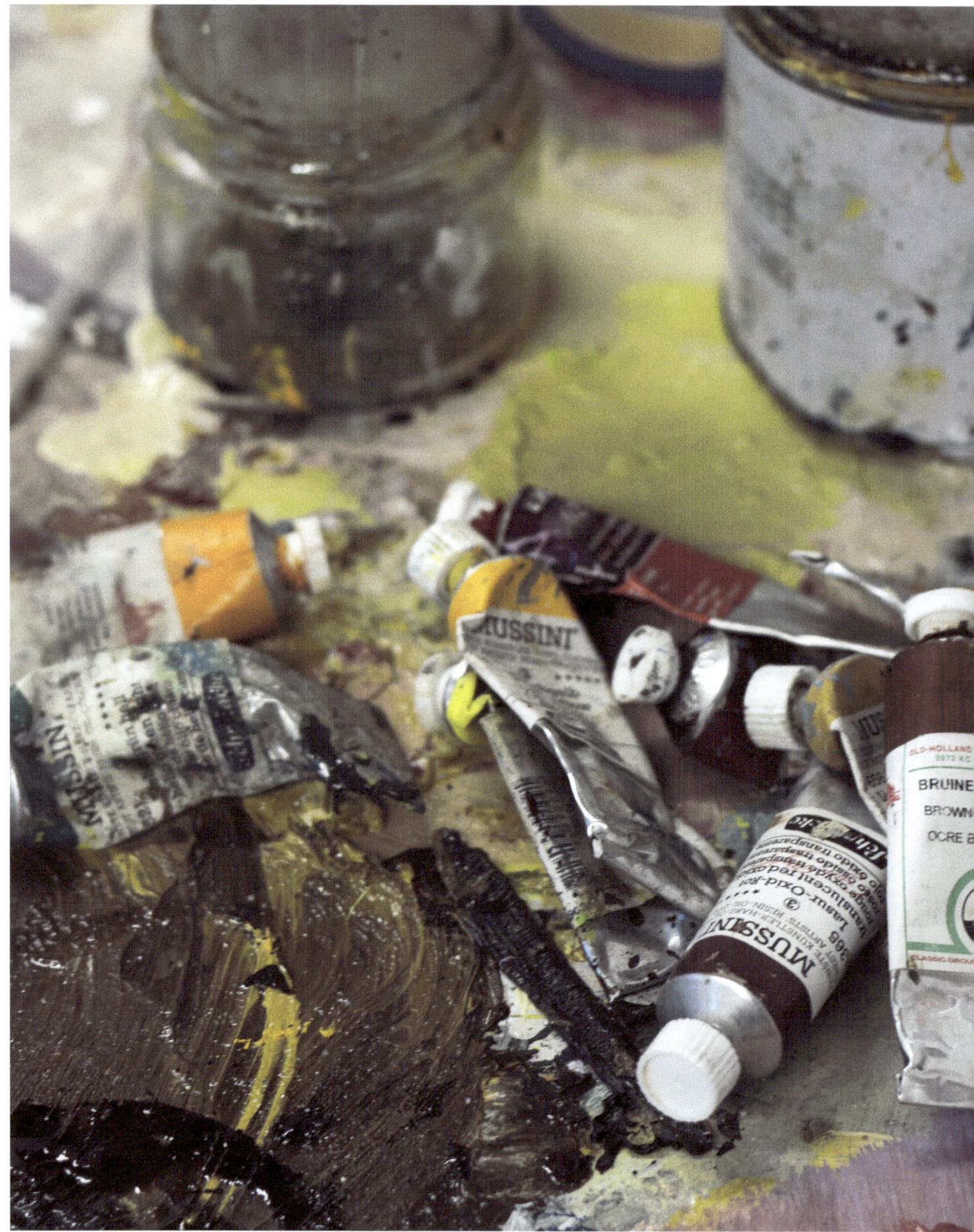

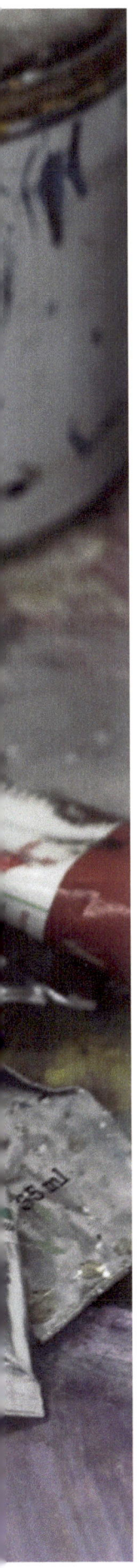

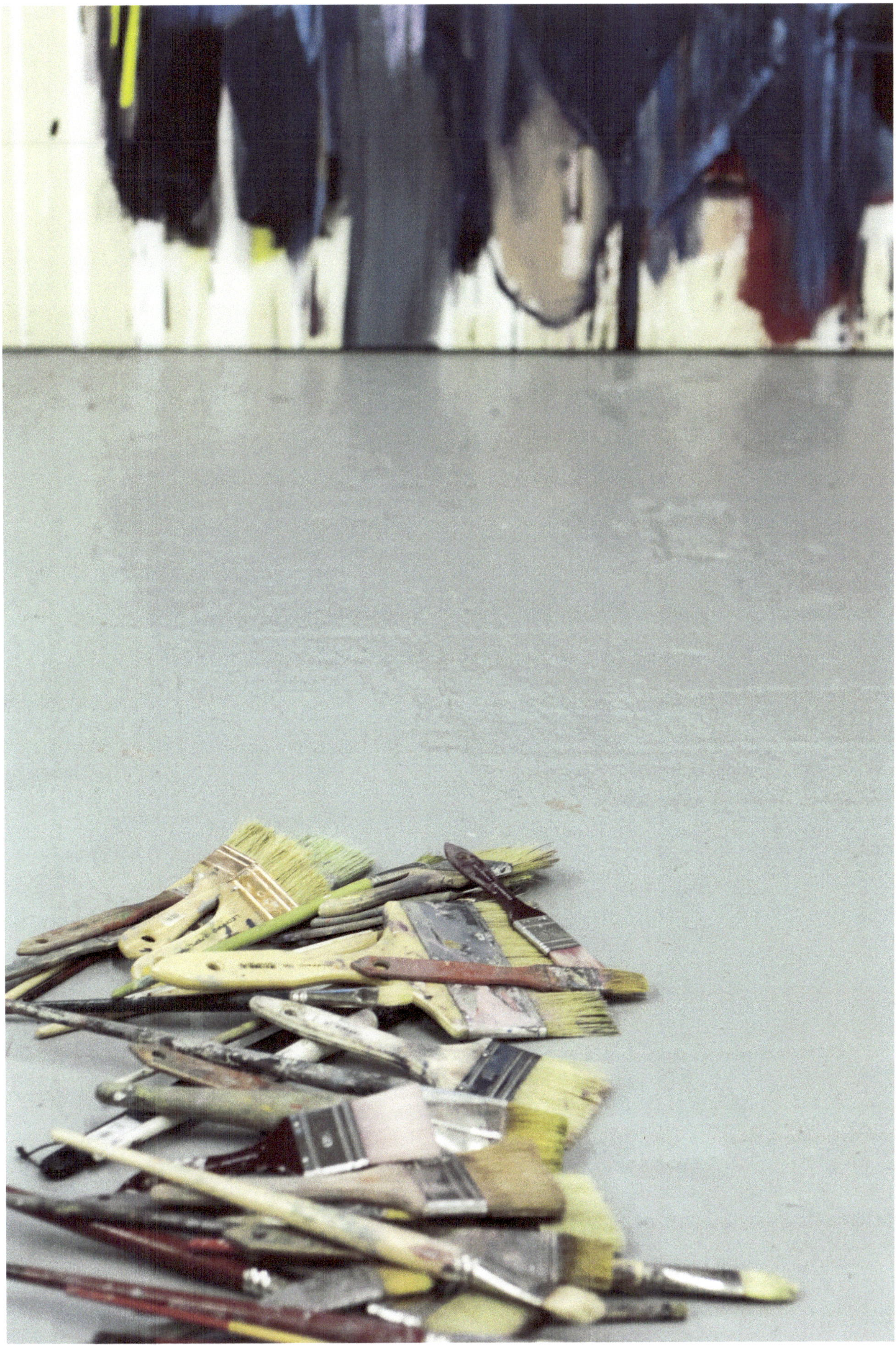

Biographies

Roy Sonnema

Foreword

Roy Sonnema received his Ph.D. in Art History and Art Criticism from the University of California at Berkeley. He has taught art history and art theory at California State University-Fullerton, Georgia Southern University, and Colorado State University. He has researched and published scholarly work in areas of contemporary art, native north American art, and seventeenth-century studies. For twelve years he served as the art critic for the Pueblo Chieftain newspaper. He is currently Professor of Art at Eastern Washington University, where he also serves as dean of the College of Arts & Letters.

Georgia Tiffany

Essay

Justin Molloy

Design

Georgia Tiffany, a native of Spokane, Washington, holds graduate degrees from Indiana University and the University of Idaho. Recipient of grants from the Washington Commission for the Humanities and the National Endowment for the Arts, she serves as a visiting scholar for the Idaho libraries "Let's Talk About It" program. Her work has appeared or is forthcoming in various anthologies and magazines including *Midwest Review*, *Willow Springs*, *Poets of the American West*, *Expose*, *Chautauqua Literary Review*, *Lost Coast Review*, *Hubbub*, *Threepenny Review*, and *Agenda*. Her chapbook, *Cut from the Score*, was published by Night Owl Press. She now lives in Moscow, Idaho.

Justin Molloy has been active in both design, technology, and research based projects for over twenty years. For the last five years he has worked for SEGD (Society for Experiential Graphic Design) as their Director of Education and Creative Director. He has organized over thirty design conferences in his tenure with the organization and has presented his design research and teaching at internationally recognized venues. Justin also manages SIGNITECTURE, a design research studio focusing on information design for the built environment. He holds a Master of Architecture from Columbia University and has held academic appointments teaching experience design in Oklahoma, Cincinnati, Illinois, Idaho, and France.

Contents